Forfaiting

FORFAITING

An alternative approach
to export trade finance

Ian Guild & Rhodri Harris

Universe Books
New York

Published in the United States of America in 1986
by Universe Books
381 Park Avenue South, New York, N.Y. 10016

86 87 88 89 90 / 10 9 8 7 6 5 4 3 2 1

Library of Congress Cataloging in Publication Data
Guild, Ian.
   Forfaiting: an alternative approach to export trade
finance.

   Includes index.
   1. Export credit. I. Harris, Rhodri. II. Title.
HG3753.G84 1985   382'.63   85-14135
ISBN 0-87663-488-9

Preface

It is the case with any specialised activity that it acquires a certain mystique which appears impenetrable to the outsider. This is as true of the financial world as of any other: it is particularly true of forfaiting.

In the case of forfaiting, there are probably two principal reasons for this – its comparatively recent development and the small number of people who are active in the à forfait market which is itself confined to the financial markets in relatively few centres in the world. These points are demonstrated by the remarkable fact that forfaiting is still not widely practised in the United States of America even though that country is the largest commercial market in the world, has one of the most sophisticated financial markets in the world and is generally known for its rapid assimilation and development of any new techniques.

It is the aim of this book to help to demystify the subject. Because of its intrinsic virtues, we believe that a greater understanding of forfaiting will lead to its increased use in the inevitable burgeoning of international trade. It is not surprising, therefore, that the Institute of Bankers in Britain has incorporated forfaiting very specifically in the syllabus for its specialist paper 'International Finance and Investment' which forms part of its examinations for the International Banking Diploma. We hope that this book will be helpful to the Institute's students as well, of course, as to exporters, importers, bankers involved in international trade and anyone who may have an interest in the subject: in so far as it assists in the development of the à forfait business, its production will have been worth while.

The essence of the book is that it should appeal to both those who might provide and those who might use à forfait finance. Thus, it starts with a description of forfaiting, and a look at its brief history and the characteristics of à forfait transactions. It discusses the advantages and disadvantages of à forfait to the various parties to a transaction and compares it with other forms of export finance and then decribes in some detail the various stages of a typical forfaiting transaction. It deals with some legal matters arising in the business and which will exercise the mind of any financier entering into an à forfait transaction. A later chapter describes legal questions which have arisen in particular instances, with a view to extracting lessons for the forfaiter.

There are chapters on the risks to the users and the providers of à forfait finance and on methods of controlling those risks. The book deals, too, with discounting methods and calculations used in forfaiting and provides at-a-glance tables translating 'straight discount' quotations into yields. Costs involved in obtaining à forfait finance and the tax implications of and appropriate accounting for forfaiting from the points of view of the users and the forfaiters are outlined. Finally, the book provides examples of the documents used in typical transactions, and management reports a forfaiter might need.

August 1985   Ian Guild
                                                                Rhodri Harris

Acknowledgements

We are most grateful for the help and encouragement we have received from family, friends and colleagues in producing this book. In particular, we acknowledge the assistance of Mr John Skelton of Withers, the London solicitors, who reviewed those sections concerned particularly with legal matters.

Contents

1

Origin and development of forfaiting

Definition

Those who are involved in the à forfait market tend to be somewhat dismissive of their business. To them it seems curious that even sophisticated businessmen seek a definition of forfaiting, since, fundamentally, forfaiting is the discounting of bills of exchange or promissory notes or other evidence of debt and, as such, is almost as old an activity as the provision of finance itself: certainly, the City of London has been discounting merchants' acceptances and receivables for many hundreds of years.

However, forfaiting warrants a rather more detailed definition than this, if only because the discounting takes place without recourse to the party from whom the debt instrument is purchased. The terms *à forfait* in French, *Forfaitierung* in German, *forfetizzazione* in Italian and *forfetización* in Spanish all involve the surrender of rights and the surrender of the right of recourse is fundamental. Forfaiting, then, is the purchase, without recourse to any previous holder of the instruments, of debt instruments due to mature in the future and arising from the provision of goods and services.

Note that the above definition refers to goods and services although, in practice, most à forfait transactions involve goods, and that it does not imply export transactions though most deals do involve them: indeed, this book will refer consistently to export transactions hereafter.

The question immediately arises as to how the seller of the debt instrument, for example a bill of exchange, denies recourse to him by the buyer. The answer is that, in endorsing the instrument to the buyer, he includes the words 'without recourse'. (The legal implications of this are considered in Chapter 4.) The objective is to pass all the risks and responsibilities of collecting the debt to the forfaiter.

The other obvious advantage, of course, to the seller is the receipt of cash today in return for money due in the future. The buyer discounts the debt instrument at an appropriate rate and pays over immediately a sum net of the discount for the whole period to maturity. Credit granted becomes cash received. Provided that the exporter has sold a validly prepared debt instrument, validly guaranteed, or avalised (see page 3), if applicable, his responsibilities in respect of the transaction have ended.

Debt instruments forfaited

Henceforth, this book will generally refer to bills of exchange and promissory notes as the debt instruments involved in forfaiting transactions. However, there are others which can be forfaited. The important point to appreciate is that, whatever the debt instruments forfaited, the forfaiter will insist that they be 'clean'. This means that they must be abstract obligations which he can rely upon absolutely. In other words, there must be no reference on the documents to any underlying trade contract upon whose performance payment is contingent. Any contract disputes affect the exporter and the importer and the forfaiter cannot be involved. He must be able to receive payment without dispute or delay.

Bill of exchange and promissory note

A bill of exchange is drawn by the seller of the goods on the buyer and accepted by the buyer as his obligation. A promissory note, on the other hand, is a promise by the buyer to pay the seller. Both these forms of payment obligation have long been in use throughout the world. Indeed, they probably originated in the Middle Ages. Because of their history, they are well known to traders and bankers and are very easily transferred from the one to the other. Consequently they tend to produce quick and simple transactions by avoiding unexpected complications.

Quite apart from this advantage, or perhaps because of it, there is one other principal reason to explain the predominant use of these two debt instruments in forfaiting transactions. The Geneva Conference of 1930 established the International Convention for Commercial Bills by which signatory countries agreed a legal framework for them. This involves a code of practice adopted into the laws of most trading nations. Not all countries were signatories: the United Kingdom, for example, was not, but the practical implications of this for UK traders or bankers are not really significant. The important point is that the Convention itself has added to the domination of bills of exchange and promissory notes as debt instruments.

The technical differences between both of these forms are considered in Chapter 4.

Book receivables and letter of credit

Letter of credit obligations and book receivables may also be forfaited. However, they are not commonly found because they lead to great complexity in negotiating the forfaiting transaction. This is an enormous disadvantage since two of the most valuable characteristics of the à forfait business are the speed with which transactions can be agreed and the simplicity of their documentation. The complexity arises because all the conditions of the transaction need to be set out in detail, which inevitably results in legal and procedural complications.

From the point of view of the forfaiter, however, the principal disadvantage arises because he will usually be providing medium-term finance (up to about seven years but sometimes more) and will insist that, whatever the debt instrument, payment for the goods or services provided must be due in periodic instalments. Consequently, the debt to be forfaited will consist of a series of payments, for example a series of ten payments of approximately equal amounts at six-monthly intervals. The forfaiter will deem this desirable partly because it avoids the shock to the debtor and guarantor of one enormous repayment and thus should facilitate repayment out of cash flow but also because it reduces the average life of the debt and therefore the forfaiter's risks.

Where bills of exchange or promissory notes are used, each repayment instalment can be evidenced by a separate document, each easily transferable and individually negotiable should the forfaiter wish to sell them to another party. Where book receivables or letters of credit are used, all maturities will be incorporated in a single document made out in favour of the beneficiary, often not transferable without the specific permission of the debtor and therefore severely restricted as to negotiability.

Guarantees

Because a forfaiter purchases debt instruments without recourse to the seller, he is bearing all the risks of non-payment by the debtor. This is fundamental to forfaiting. Unless the debtor is a first-class company or institution of unquestionable ability to pay, the forfaiter will seek some security for the debt. This will take the form of an 'aval' or an unconditional or irrevocable guarantee in a form and by a bank or state organisation acceptable to the forfaiter. This will be the forfaiter's sole security for the debt and thus will be a *sine qua non* of the à forfait transaction. Apart from reducing the forfaiter's risks, this security facilitates the resale of the discounted paper to other forfaiters – 'secondary market' business (see page 5). If a bank aval or guarantee is obtained, the bank will normally be international though resident in the importer's country. Sometimes, however, offshore banks will be used: the important point is that the guarantor will need to be able to assess the debtor's credit-worthiness.

Chapter 4 considers the forms this security might take and certain technical and legal questions related to it.

Origins of forfaiting

The purchase of debt instruments without recourse to the seller is, in the main, a phenomenon of the period since the Second World War. The Zurich banking community, long experienced in international trade finance and with a wide reputation in banking, pioneered it to finance the purchase of grain sold by the United States to East European countries.

Although, therefore, commodity-based transactions gave birth to the business, its characteristics were soon seen to be suitable for the emerging international business in capital goods. In the late 1950s and 1960s, the supply of these goods and, therefore, competition between suppliers grew so that buyers increasingly demanded credit periods exceeding the traditional 90 or 180 days. As international trade barriers fell and many African, Asian and Latin American countries developed their trading activities, West European exporters found it increasingly difficult to provide credit from their own resources at the same time as funding the heavy internal investment necessary in order to take advantage of these new markets.

Development of the à forfait market

Forfaiting has now become established in financial centres other than Switzerland. More à forfait business is now conducted, probably, in London than anywhere else. In that London is a larger centre than any in Switzerland, this change is perhaps not surprising.

Certainly, exports of various European countries have long been financed from London, and 'the City' has historically not been slow to exploit any new financing techniques. But there is a technical reason, too, that has enabled London to gain a competitive edge on Switzerland in the à forfait market: Swiss finance companies are liable to a stamp duty on negotiable instruments each time they are bought or sold. This is not to say that Switzerland, and Zurich particularly, is not still a major à forfait centre but it is now probably second to London. It is also worth noting that a great deal of business originates in West Germany.

As forfaiting has increasingly been offered in various financial centres in Europe (though seldom elsewhere in the world), so the amount of business conducted has grown. It would, however, be a mistake to equate this expansion simply with an increase in the number of forfaiting centres. In fact, the growth probably owes more to increases in the risks to which exporters are exposed and the lack of adequate alternative sources of finance dealing with those risks. In addition, of course, à forfait finance has intrinsic virtues which make it an attractive form of medium-term finance in its own right: these are discussed in Chapter 2, where forfaiting is also compared with other financing methods.

Specifically, the exporter is now subject to loss from adverse movement in interest rates and currency parities to a much greater degree than hitherto simply because the flow of funds between major trading countries is now far freer than traditionally was the case. For example, the United Kingdom has abandoned both exchange controls and fixed currency rates in recent years. This has made any form of finance offering a fixed interest rate to the exporter and removing the risks of currency fluctuations from him more attractive than ever: these are both characteristics of forfaiting.

In addition, there continue to be sovereign and transfer risks attached to exporting. In particular, many lesser-developed countries are chronically short of hard currency to pay for exports whatever the liquid position of the importer himself. This political risk has tended to grow rather than diminish over the years as the recurrent requests by many nations to reschedule their international debts eloquently testify. Again, forfaiting scores in this regard because the forfaiter accepts the political and transfer risks attached to any debt that he purchases. As the insurance premiums on Government-backed schemes such as those of the Export Credits Guarantee Department and on private schemes, when they are available, have increased in the light of these political developments, and the conditions attached to such schemes have become more restrictive, so this aspect of forfaiting has been perceived more and more as a principal reason for taking this form of finance. This trend has been accentuated as the risks accepted by such insurance schemes have declined in terms both of amount involved and of countries covered.

As to the services provided by the à forfait market, recent years have seen three principal developments.

The secondary market and investment in forfaited assets

As soon as a forfaiter has purchased forfaited assets, he has, of course, made an investment. It will usually be, by the nature of à forfait business, at least in part, a medium-term investment. The forfaiter may not wish to tie his resources up in that investment for that period and may therefore seek an opportunity to resell the investment to someone who becomes the forfaiter instead. Those who trade in this way operate what is known as a 'secondary market'. Note that the first forfaiter may wish to resell only a part of the asset he has acquired: the nature of a forfaited asset makes splitting it up like this a simple matter, since, as earlier stated, it will generally consist of a series of bills of exchange or promissory notes maturing at varying times in the future. One or more of these individual notes or bills – tranches – may be sold.

The secondary market in à forfait paper, particularly in London, is now very active. As forfaiting has grown, so this market has developed. It would be mistaken to think of it as entirely separate from the primary market, since several forfaiters are active in both: in other words, they on-sell some paper but also maintain an investment portfolio of à forfait paper themselves. However, some forfaiters make a point of being end-investors rather than traders in à forfait paper, while some forfaiters deal little in the primary market, making their money from 'turns' on trading the paper. That this diversity exists is perhaps the most telling evidence of the increasing maturity of forfaiting.

There are also instances of individuals purchasing à forfait paper for private investment purposes recognising that the yields on the particular bills or notes purchased are higher than they could obtain with similar risk, or relative lack of risk, elsewhere. An individual, like any dealer on the secondary market, may find that, for reasons of confidentiality explained below, his source will not physically release the paper to him or give him any details of the transaction other than the amounts, maturity dates, issuer and guarantor. The forfaiter from whom he is purchasing will, in such circumstances, collect payment upon maturity and transfer funds to him.

Why is the purchase of à forfait paper in the secondary market surrounded by such secrecy?

An exporter will sometimes expect that the forfaiter will be circumspect in any trading that he does. After all, an exporter will be concerned to protect his relationship with his customers and may not want those customers to see that he needs to finance his receivables. This will be particularly true if the contract whose payment is the subject of the à forfait finance was difficult to obtain because the terms of the finance were long and tortuous to agree: reselling of à forfait paper carries an implicit recognition that its yield is attractive.

In addition, an exporter is unlikely to be pleased if he is approached by a third party with respect to his financing arrangements. Any sale of à forfait paper in the secondary market carries the risk that this involuntary widening of his business relationships will occur. For the same reason, an exporter will try to ensure that paper he has sold does not circulate in a market which he cannot supervise or influence.

Even if the exporter is relaxed about the resale of his obligations, his own bank may not be. The bank may fear, or suspect, that any forfaiter will try to broaden his relationships with his client, thereby endangering his own position: since many forfaiters are a department or a subsidiary of a bank, this new relationship might not stop at forfaiting. It is true that this is protectionism, but the à forfait market has to be alert and, indeed, sympathetic to the susceptibilities of the banking community since the whole business depends upon trust and goodwill.

The consequence of all this is that exporters may well seek to impose restrictions or exclusions upon forfaiters by specific contractual terms which make the à forfait paper very difficult to transfer. It is usually possible to find ways to avoid such restrictions, for example by fiduciary handling of the paper or undisclosed assignments, but they add complication and legal risk to what should be a simple transaction and, therefore, forfaiters are seldom prepared to use them.

Instead, forfaiters try to avoid contractual restrictions by protecting confidentiality, since exporters can require that forfaited paper will not be passed around the market but will remain with the primary forfaiter: indeed, any forfaiter specifically asked by an exporter not to resell the paper he has purchased will give that undertaking and honour it. Of course, the corollary of this policy is that the primary forfaiter may be the only party in a position to send the forfaited paper for payment at maturity and to collect and transfer the money. This emphasises his responsibility for checking and confirming the validity of the paper itself and of any guarantee, or aval. This latter aspect is considered more fully in Chapter 4. These functions and the holding of the paper until maturity are carried out free of charge.

Because of the possible lack of information available to them and because à forfait transactions are generally very large, so that only a substantial investment portfolio can assume the risks attendant upon the purchase of forfaited assets, individuals investing in them are few in number. Any secondary market dealer must obviously trust the seller of the paper implicitly and, conversely, the forfaiter will be careful in selling on the secondary market since he will not want problems in the future from purchases under a misconception as to the workings of the à forfait market. In particular, when bills of exchange are on-sold, there is a technical legal difficulty as to the effectiveness of the 'without recourse' endorsement on them (as explained more fully in Chapter 4) so that the seller will want to be sure that he can take the purchaser at his word when he agrees not to attempt to claim recourse against him. In addition, the seller will be most anxious to be certain that the purchaser, the new forfaiter, is able to withstand the loss should it not prove possible to obtain payment at maturity.

Despite these constraints, there is a flourishing secondary market. It is easy to see why if one considers the reasons which might persuade a primary forfaiter to resell on the secondary market and a trader or investor to purchase on the secondary market.

A primary forfaiter might well find that the purchase of a particular transaction fills the credit limits he has imposed for the country whose guarantee backs the paper. Any subsequent transactions he is offered with that country risk, however attractive the yield, he must reject if he is not to exceed his limit. The obvious response to this dilemma is to resell either the paper he bought earlier or the transaction he is now offered. The same applies if it is not the country limits which provide the constraint but the limits he will have set for holdings of paper backed by a particular guarantor or the maximum amount of borrowing he can obtain to fund his portfolio of à forfait paper.

Apart from these possibilities, a primary forfaiter might be attracted into reselling on the secondary market simply because interest rates have fallen so that any secondary purchaser will be prepared to accept a lower discount than that implicit in the original purchase by the primary buyer. In other words, he will be happy to accept a capital profit on resale: if this is his motivation, he will probably be expecting that the reduction in interest rates generally which has led to the opportunity to sell at a profit is a temporary phenomenon so that he will, in the fairly near future, be able to replenish his portfolio with assets with as good or better a yield than the asset he is selling. This is, of course, a matter of judgement and, to a large extent, a matter of luck, too.

There are other possible reasons for a primary forfaiter to resell à forfait paper. For example, he might simply want liquidity in the expectation of changing interest rates or in order to take advantage of a chance to purchase higher-yielding or less risky paper bearing a different country or guarantor risk. Or, more simply, a buyer may appear on the secondary market offering a particularly favourable price for his paper: in this case, the purchaser will effectively be taking a view of the risk value of the paper or of the probable future interest-rate movements slightly different from that of the seller so that he is prepared to accept the paper at a lower discount than the primary forfaiter is receiving.

For the secondary market forfaiter, there are two principal attractions of the market. First, the yield on à forfait paper tends to exceed that available in the fixed-rate securities market from assets of comparable risk with similar terms to maturity in the same currencies. This recognises the fact that forfaited assets represent the provision of fixed-rate trade finance and, as such, enjoy a premium. It also arises in part from the premium inevitably attached to the expertise of the primary forfaiters and the speed and simplicity of documentation with which they are able to offer that trade finance. Second, any investor is concerned to minimise his risks and the security of first-class bank avals or guarantees supporting forfaited assets is as good as he could expect to find.

However, despite the attractions of à forfait paper as investments, it is very likely that a secondary market forfaiter will be quite prepared to resell the assets himself if he sees an appropriate opportunity to do so. In deciding whether or not to resell, he will be considering factors very similar to those applicable to the primary forfaiter and outlined above. But it must be emphasised that trading opportunities in the flourishing secondary forfaiting market do not exist in the same way as they do in the equity or gilt-edged securities markets. The volumes transacted and the number of forfaiters are still too small. Consequently, the secondary market has not yet matured to the extent of becoming a broker's market with middlemen executing quick-fire buying and selling trades. Many forfaiters, particularly those operating in the primary market, are anxious that such a development should not take place since they believe that it will tend to frighten away exporters and their banks fearing the lack of commitment and lack of control over paper and, therefore, obligations that it represents, though it would be a brave, or foolish, man who denies the possibility that it will happen.

Syndications

Another fairly recent development in forfaiting has been the syndication of individual asset purchases. As transactions subject to forfaiting agreements tend to involve large sums of money and therefore large commitments on a particular guarantee from a particular bank in a particular country, syndication is often an obvious move in just the same way as much of today's commercial lending is done on a syndicated basis. Quite apart from the self-evident differences between these two forms of finance, however, there is an important distinction between the publicity surrounding syndicated commercial lending and the lack of publicity in an à forfait transaction. While a syndicated commercial loan will probably be publicised in one or more national newspapers by full-page 'tombstone' advertisements listing all the parties to the deal, nothing will appear in print regarding the à forfait deal – welcome reticence from the exporter's point of view.

In practice, the syndication will be arranged quite simply by a forfaiter contacting others and arriving at an agreement whereby each forfaiter will purchase different tranches of the forfaited obligation. Generally, different bills or notes will be bought by different forfaiters, but, if the amounts involved are very large, even individual bills or notes may occasionally be split by the issuance of participation letters and spread between the forfaiters. Alternatively, provided that the exporter is prepared to arrange this, the number of forfaited documents may be increased, and therefore each reduced in amount, by changing the frequency of maturity. For example, instead of maturities at the normal six-monthly intervals, they may be scheduled at three-monthly or even more frequent intervals.

Incidentally, instances where different forfaiters participate in the same tranches of an obligation rather than purchase different bills or notes are not generally favoured by the market as a whole because they involve side agreements between the participants. This not only destroys the simplicity so characteristic of forfaiting but also restricts the transferability of the assets involved, thus almost inevitably removing the possibility of sales to the secondary market. In addition, the precise legal status of such side agreements in concert with bills of exchange and promissory notes has yet to be tested.

The important point to grasp is that there is a fundamental difference between a forfaiter involved in a syndicated obligation and one purchasing in the secondary market, although both may obtain only a part of the obligation itself. In the first case, the forfaiter is a primary market purchaser with the responsibility to check the validity both of the bills or notes he has bought and of the guarantee or aval attached to them. These duties have legal significance as explained further in Chapter 4. The purchaser in the secondary market does not have them.

Variable-rate finance

The third recent development which needs to be discussed is the increasing provision via forfaiting of variable-rate finance. This is a response to the increased volatility of interest rates and mirrors the reluctance of many banks to enter into fixed-rate interest arrangements.

From the point of view of the exporter, any sale of his debts at a variable discount defeats a principal objective of his obtaining the finance in the first place. Not surprisingly, therefore, this development affects the secondary market not the primary. What happens is that a primary forfaiter sells some paper into the secondary market at a price reflecting a discount based upon prevailing interest rates, with the provision that there will be a financial adjustment at a fixed future date to take account of subsequent interest-rate movements. In fact, there may be such adjustments at a number of different dates throughout the period to the maturity of the bills or notes.

From the point of view of either party, this sort of agreement contains the risk of substantial future payments which can only be quantified at the agreed recalculation dates. The existence of such a contingent liability will, of course, be of concern to any forfaiter and his auditor, and it is probably true to say that its inherent danger and the fact that it contradicts the perceived objective of forfaiting to provide fixed-rate finance have made forfaiters unwilling to do more than a small percentage of their secondary market business on this basis.

Constraints upon the speed of growth of the market

There appears no cause at present to suppose that the reasons outlined above for the growth of the market in recent years will cease to be true in the foreseeable future. However, there are constraints upon the entry of new forfaiters to the market.

The constraints are three-fold. First, it is a specialised technique requiring expert personnel. There are few such people and expertise takes years to develop. Second, though there are large numbers of banks from the United States with an international presence, few have yet ventured into the à forfait market. One of the major reasons for this also applies to international banks from other countries: à forfait finance is transaction-related and does not of itself provide a spin-off in the form of the provision of other banking services for an exporter or necessarily even other à forfait transactions for him.

Third, this is fixed-rate finance and a number of major banks in both Europe and the United States have burnt their fingers badly in recent years in the provision of fixed-rate lending and are anxious to avoid anything that smacks of it. Since this is medium-term finance – up to seven years or more – banks often find it difficult to match the maturity dates of the assets forfaited with their own borrowing so that there is a residual risk in the event of interest-rate movements and this exposure does seem to have inhibited them from venturing into the market.

The consequence of these constraints is that banks have tended not to market forfaiting so that demand for à forfait finance has not developed to its full potential. In other words, many exporters remain unaware of the possibilities provided by forfaiting for satisfying their medium-term credit requirements. In that this is an artificial limitation to the growth of forfaiting, it must ultimately be removed: commercial banks, in particular, can be expected to introduce forfaiting to their clients increasingly in years to come.

Size of the à forfait market

Any estimate of the total size of the à forfait market is no more than a guess. As already stated, the market has grown considerably in recent years but remains only a very small proportion of the total medium-term finance provided world-wide. Perhaps there exists approximately US$10 billion of à forfait paper today, approximately 30% of which is being traded at any moment.

2

Characteristics of an
à forfait transaction

Types of trade financed via forfaiting

In Chapter 1, it was explained that the origins of forfaiting lay in East–West trade in the aftermath of the Second World War. At the start, debts for commodities such as grain were forfaited but this soon developed into the forfaiting of payment obligations for capital goods. Apart from a growth in the number of transactions available to forfaiters from this expansion in the types of trade subject to à forfait finance, the most obvious change was in the period of credit which was extended. Commodity transactions were and still are financed for periods seldom exceeding six months. Capital goods transactions tend to be financed for much longer periods – typically five to seven years although the period often extends well beyond this, ten years not being uncommon.

Nowadays, forfaiting is associated mainly with medium-term credit for capital goods. This leads to the familiar heresy that this is the only type of transaction which can be forfaited. In fact, à forfait finance is increasingly used for non-capital goods exports and for financing the provision of services rather than goods. Indeed, it is broadly true that virtually any export sale can be à forfait financed.

Size of à forfait transactions

A second heresy, or old wives' tale perhaps, is widely held. This is that à forfait transactions must be of very high value. This again is derived from forfaiting's association with the export of capital goods. It is certainly true that most à forfait finance, both in terms of the amount of finance provided and in the number of transactions financed, is advanced for high-value transactions, that is, exports of over US$1 million. However, it is easily possible to obtain à forfait finance for transactions of no more than

US$100,000. Naturally, the discount rate offered by a forfaiter for any transaction of as little as this will tend to include a larger premium than that sought for higher-value transactions, but this merely reflects the fact that the work involved in the quotation for a low-value transaction, checking the documentation and collecting is probably as great as that needing to be performed by the forfaiter in a much larger transaction. It is worth stressing, too, that even smaller transactions than this are sometimes forfaited and that, conversely, there is no upper limit to the value of à forfait transactions although any exceeding about US$50 million will almost certainly be syndicated, as explained in Chapter 1.

Currencies involved in à forfait transactions

The third common misconception about forfaiting is that only transactions in US dollars, Deutschmarks and Swiss francs are suitable for it. This belief has arisen in part from its history but also because these currencies have long been traded internationally and have shown stability, indeed usually strength, in the increasingly volatile currency world. It remains the case that most à forfait transactions do involve one of these three currencies and that the à forfait market tends to use US dollars in abstract discussions. However, transactions in many other currencies have been forfaited in recent years, particularly in Japanese yen, Dutch guilders, sterling and Swedish krona: indeed, forfaiting can be used wherever medium-term forward currency markets are available. The only real constraint upon the currency of a transaction is that it should be readily transferable between countries, although, where the currency is little traded, then the forfaiter might well be prepared to provide finance for only the short term, perhaps 12 to 18 months.

Essential prerequisites of an à forfait transaction

From the above, it should be apparent that forfaiting is a flexible tool in international finance. Essentially there are very few prerequisites of a transaction which can be forfaited.

1. An exporter will have agreed to extend credit to his customer for some period of between six months and ten years, or perhaps longer.
2. The exporter will have agreed to stage the payment of his receivable so that the bills of exchange or promissory notes or other instruments evidencing the debt will typically be a series (for example, ten due six-monthly over five years).
3. Unless the importer is a Government agency or a multinational company, repayment of the debts will be avalised or guaranteed unconditionally and irrevocably by a bank or state institution acceptable to the forfaiter.

Advantages and disadvantages of à forfait finance

Advantages to the exporter

1. À forfait finance is fixed-rate finance.
2. Finance is provided by the forfaiter without recourse to the exporter.
3. The exporter receives cash immediately he delivers the goods or provides the services. This results in business liquidity, reducing bank borrowing or freeing financial resources for reinvestment or other purposes.
4. The exporter need spend no time or money in administering or collecting his debts.
5. The forfaiter, not the exporter, bears the risks of currency and interest-rate movements and the credit risks associated with sovereign default and the failure of the guarantor.
6. À forfait finance is negotiable for each of the exporter's trade transactions: he does not need to commit all of his business or any significant part of it.
7. The exporter can ascertain very quickly whether a forfaiter is prepared to extend finance for any given transaction. In fact, provided that the guarantor is acceptable to the forfaiter, the financial terms of the finance can be agreed within hours.
8. Because the finance is generally provided against such straightforward debt instruments as bills of exchange and promissory notes, all documentation is simple and can be quickly compiled.
9. À forfait transactions are confidential, unlike, for example, commercial loans where 'tombstone' advertisements are commonplace.
10. The exporter can obtain an advance option to finance at a fixed rate from the forfaiter. He can therefore build financing costs into his contract price and quote a figure including the CIF cost of his goods, the costs of the credit and, if necessary, the costs of any foreign exchange cover he needs to take to swap into his own currency the currency he agrees to charge the importer.

Disadvantages to the exporter

1. As considered further in Chapter 4, the exporter has a responsibility to ensure that the debt instruments are validly prepared and guaranteed so that there can be no recourse to him in the event of default by the guarantor. He should be conversant, therefore, with the regulations of the importing country as to the form of bills of exchange or promissory notes and guarantees or avals. In practice, however, the responsibility in this respect is generally assumed by the forfaiter.

2. The exporter may have difficulty in ensuring that the importer can obtain a guarantor satisfactory to the forfaiter.
3. Because he is accepting all the risks, the forfaiter will expect a higher margin than normally sought by a commercial lender on similar business. This must not, however, be exaggerated, as competition between the various forms of trade finance and between forfaiters keeps the disparity down. In addition, the exporter does not have the cost of the insurance cover, for example via the Export Credits Guarantee Department, which he will otherwise take out as security for extending credit himself.

Advantages to the importer

1. Documentation of the transaction is simple and quickly compiled.
2. The importer obtains fixed-rate extended credit.
3. Borrowing to pay immediately for his purchases will use up his credit lines: although the bank guarantee he takes will also count against his available credit, it will generally do so to a lesser degree.

Disadvantages to the importer

1. As noted above, the bank aval or guarantee he will usually need will probably count to some degree against his credit lines.
2. The importer will have to pay a guarantee fee.
3. The legal position of bills of exchange and promissory notes which a forfaiter will accept is clear: they are 'abstract' documents giving an absolute obligation to pay. Therefore, any dispute concerning the goods purchased is irrelevant to the payment for them. Payment cannot legally be withheld, so that the importer, in the event of such a dispute, will need to seek recompense from the exporter.

   To mitigate his exposure in this respect, however, an importer will sometimes impose conditions upon the payment of a small proportion of the contract value and this proportion will not be forfaited.
4. The higher margins sought by forfaiters are a disadvantage to the importer as well as the exporter.

Advantages to the forfaiter

1. Again, documentation is simple and quickly compiled: there are no 30-page loan agreements as in commercial lending.
2. The assets purchased are easily transferable as to title so that trading them in the secondary market is possible.
3. Although the higher margins associated with à forfait finance are a disadvantage to the exporter and importer, they are naturally attractive to the forfaiter.

Disadvantages to the forfaiter

1. The forfaiter has no recourse to anyone else in the event of a default in repayment.
2. As is the case for the exporter, the forfaiter must know the laws and regulations governing the validity of bills of exchange, promissory notes, guarantees or avals in the various countries with whom his exporter clients will be conducting business. Chapter 10 considers the legal position of the forfaiter who fails to obtain valid bills or notes validly guaranteed or avalised.
3. The forfaiter also bears the responsibility for checking the credit-worthiness of the guarantor.
4. The forfaiter cannot accelerate payment of bills or notes which have yet to mature merely because a bill or note of the series which has matured has not been paid. Such acceleration clauses are a standard feature of ordinary commercial loan agreements, but the legal position of bills and notes virtually precludes similar treatment for them.
5. The forfaiter bears all funding and interest-rate risks and these risks exist during the option and commitment periods (explained further in Chapter 3) as well as during the periods to maturity of the bills or notes. This is far more significant an exposure than is the case in commercial lending because most commercial lending today bears a variable interest rate.

Disadvantages 2 and 3 above for the forfaiter are not, of course, exclusive to him. Any financier needs to check the credit-worthiness and bona fides of his debtor and to ensure that all documentation surrounding the transaction to which he has committed himself is satisfactory. These are listed as particular disadvantages to the forfaiter, however, because there are no hefty loan agreements prepared by lawyers or additional security which he can fall back on. While simple, quickly compiled documentation is, therefore, an advantage in most respects, it does leave a greater onus on the forfaiter.

It must also be appreciated that the forfaiter bears sovereign, political and transfer risks and the risks of currency fluctuations, too. These are not listed as disadvantages of forfaiting, however, because any international lender has these risks.

Advantages to the guarantor

1. A guarantor has as great an interest in simple documentation as any of the other parties to the transaction.
2. The guarantor earns a fee for his services.

Disadvantage to the guarantor

There is only one disadvantage of à forfait finance, but it is important. The guarantor has an absolute obligation to pay a bill or note that he has guaranteed and, as is the case with the importer, no contract dispute surrounding the goods or services provided can absolve him from this or, indeed, delay his payment. In just the same way, however, he is absolutely entitled to reimbursement from the importer whose name also appears on the bill or note as an obligor and who, therefore, has the real exposure.

Forfaiting as an additional form of finance

It has often been assumed by those outside the à forfait market that one of the advantages of forfaiting to exporters and importers is its 'last resort' characteristic. In other words, à forfait finance can be regarded as additional to other forms of finance because, albeit for a greater cost, it can be obtained for those risks, particularly country risks, for which no other source of credit can be found.

This assumption is largely erroneous. In general, a forfaiter will be as chary of lending on poor risks as any prudent financier. In so far as it retains a grain of truth, this is only because the international nature of the secondary à forfait market and syndications within the primary market may, in some cases, permit greater opportunities to 'lay off' risk and provide greater 'placing power' than is true of, for example, state-guaranteed insurance schemes.

Comparison between forfaiting and other forms of trade finance

In producing a comparison between forfaiting and other forms of trade finance readily available today, it is necessary first of all to appreciate that an importer seeking medium-term credit or an exporter requiring finance to provide medium-term credit for his customers will have comparatively few alternatives in mind. Assuming that his credit rating is satisfactory and that he enjoys good relations with an accommodating bank, his bank manager is likely to receive his proposal first. His request for credit or an addition to his existing credit lines will doubtless be met with sympathy, and probably with helpful enthusiasm, but his bank manager will usually suggest that his borrowing interest rate be fixed for only three or six months at a time with changes in the rate to reflect alterations in market interest rates at the end of each period.

Obviously, such variable-rate borrowing will be attractive to a borrower who is confident that interest rates will tend to fall over the period for which he needs the finance. However, few bankers or economists will predict where interest rates will be in six months' time let alone in five to ten years.

In recent times, interest rates have shown greater volatility than ever before and this applies not merely to those of less stable countries but even to those of traditionally 'safe' nations such as the United States, West Germany and Switzerland. In these circumstances, it is unusual to find a borrower sure enough about future rates of interest to accept happily variable interest rates on his borrowing: and the attendant uncertainty has clearly been a constraining influence upon the willingness of traders to undertake costly expansion plans or to fund longer-term research and development projects.

Consequently, of the advantages, as detailed earlier in this chapter, enjoyed by à forfait finance from the point of view of the importer or the exporter, the most significant is likely to be the fixed interest rate it implies. Indeed, it is probably true to say that one of the reasons for the considerable increase in the use of leasing and factoring in recent years is the fixed-rate nature of the finance they supply. A comparison of à forfait with other available financing methods must, therefore, concentrate on the limited alternatives for the borrower intent on fixing his interest rates though, in so far as some of these alternatives do not immediately turn debt into cash (another very significant advantage of forfaiting), even they cannot be regarded as directly competitive in the eyes of the exporter.

Commercial borrowing

Although, as stated above, banks normally lend on a variable interest rate basis, the intrepid borrower may be able to arrange fixed-rate terms. However, the bank will extract a price in terms of the higher margin over base rates, LIBOR, etc., that it will require. In addition, the bank will probably demand security for the loan, perhaps in the form of a fixed or floating charge over the borrower's assets.

Apart from this, an exporter taking a loan will still have the risk of non-payment by his purchaser. This risk can be mitigated by insurance cover such as that provided by the Export Credits Guarantee Department, but the cover is unlikely to extend to 100% of the debt and payment will, under the terms of the policy, be delayed for, probably, at least six months, and sometimes up to 18 months (usually until legal steps for repayment have failed), although repayment to the lending bank must still be made on the due date. Remember, too, that the insurance premiums are quite expensive and becoming more so as international lending becomes more risky: indeed, cover has been withdrawn from a number of countries in the recent past.

As in the United Kingdom, where it is done via the Export Credits Guarantee Department, many countries operate 'interest make-up' schemes for specified importing countries whereby the exporter can borrow from his bank at an artificially low fixed rate, the difference between this rate and the market rate for the borrowing being paid by a Government agency. Such fixed-rate finance is normally attractive, but the exporter will still have to take out insurance cover and is still subject to the non-payment or late payment risks outlined above.

Leasing and hire purchase

These have proved very popular methods of obtaining fixed-rate finance in a number of countries, notably the United Kingdom and the United States, since the 1970s. However, they have significant limitations which mean that they cannot be regarded as directly competitive with à forfait finance for most transactions. Specifically, they are limited to the supply of capital goods, they involve complex documentation and, in order to obtain full benefit from leasing, the exporter must have taxable profits against which he can write off the cost of the assets. If his tax capacity is inadequate, the exporter may be able to arrange to sell the assets to a finance house who will enter into the leasing agreement with the importer in his stead, but any financier entering into a leasing or hire purchase agreement on behalf of the exporter will probably require the right of recourse to the exporter in the event of default by the importer.

Factoring

Factoring is another form of finance which has achieved popularity recently and it is undoubtedly true that higher borrowing costs and tightened cash flows arising from any downturn in trade in the future will emphasise this trend. Again, however, this is not truly competitive with forfaiting, principally because it is generally used for short-term receivables – 90- to 180-day trade credit. In addition, factoring can normally be obtained for debts in relatively few currencies and always leaves a residual risk to the exporter as the factoring house will usually accept only about 80% of the debt and demand recourse to him in the event of default. Also, a factor generally expects to purchase all or a substantial proportion of the exporter's debts acceptable to him. Finally, discounts in factoring tend to be high.

Variable-rate borrowing hedged by interest-rate futures

This is a new entrant to the realm of fixed-rate financing. Indeed, interest-rate futures have only been available in the United Kingdom since 1982 and in the United States, where they originated, for little longer. Consequently, the use of interest-rate futures to hedge variable-rate borrowing is in its infancy and few companies practise it.

The theory is simple enough. A borrower hedges his loan by committing to future sales of interest-bearing gilt-edged securities whose total face value equals the loan itself and which mature coincidentally with the loan. In, perhaps, six months' time, the interest rate chargeable on the loan is likely to change. If rates have increased, the future sales can be closed out at a profit equal to the discounted value of the increased loan interest cost: if rates have fallen, the loss on the forwards equals the gain on the interest cost. The process can be repeated every six months, or as often as interest rates on the borrowing are agreed to be changeable. This method of fixing interest rates is likely to increase in popularity, but it will probably always have certain limitations.

The futures instruments which can be traded are unlikely to match the exporter's borrowings in terms of the period to maturity and the currency (only US dollar and sterling interest-rate futures are available at present), so that they can only act as imperfect hedges. As significant, the effective interest rates on the medium-term instruments, when and if they become available on the futures markets, will mirror medium-term money market rates, whereas variable-rate borrowing with its interest rate changeable at six-monthly intervals will mirror short-term interest rates. It will never by these means, therefore, be possible to do better than reduce effective movements in the interest rates charged to the borrower rather than achieve a fixed rate, although the degree of stability gained may be sufficient for some borrowers. Certainly, there are great potential advantages of such a hedging mechanism – ease of buying and selling the hedges, virtually no documentation and fairly low commission rates. However, the disadvantages of commercial borrowing specified above, in terms of loan documentation and risk of default, remain.

Summary

There are few alternatives to à forfait finance. Those that do exist tend not to enjoy the advantages of forfaiting as enumerated earlier in this chapter: indeed, they tend to have specific, important limitations. In short, forfaiting scores well because it is virtually alone in providing fixed-rate finance without risk to the exporter.

3

Conducting an
à forfait transaction

Initiating the deal

Given that à forfait finance oils the wheels of international trade, there are two obvious potential initiators of an à forfait transaction – the importer and the exporter. In addition, a forfaiting company will receive requests for quotations from banks working on behalf of importers or exporters quite apart from requests from the principals themselves – after all, there are still only a small minority of international, let alone national, banks which are active on their own account in the à forfait market. In this case, the only additional point of concern to the forfaiter is to establish whether or not the bank requesting a quotation is intending to act as an agent or as a principal, that is, a primary forfaiter, in the à forfait transaction. There are important legal implications here which are discussed in Chapter 4.

None the less, the most likely initial contact that the forfaiter will have is the exporter or his bank. This is hardly surprising since the documents to be discounted will probably be either bills of exchange drawn by the exporter or promissory notes payable to him so that discounting them is inevitably very much his responsibility and also any exporter seeking a major overseas order is likely to wish to provide finance as part of the package.

This indicates the importance of involving the forfaiter at an early stage in the proceedings. Even before the exporter's contract tender has been submitted, the forfaiter can indicate whether, in principle, forfaiting is possible and what requirements as to a bank guarantee or aval he will have. He will usually go further and quote the discount rate he wants. Without at least this degree of assurance, an exporter is not really in a position to quote a firm price, including an allowance for the cost of finance, on the contract. In practice, it must be said, the exporter often does not contact the forfaiter at this early stage so that he finds, to his consternation, that the finance margin he has built into his tender price is inadequate.

Forfaiter's questions of the initiator

Once approached, and having established whether the transaction is financial or trade-backed (see Chapter 4 for an explanation of the difference), there are 12 basic questions that the forfaiter will ask.

1. *How much is to be financed, in what currency and for how long?*
2. *Who is the exporter and in what country is he situated?* This question is important despite the fact that finance is provided without recourse to the exporter because, as discussed in Chapter 4, there are circumstances in which the forfaiter can claim on the exporter whose bona fides and credit-worthiness are therefore significant. The exporter's credibility is important, too, in helping to ensure that the export contract is completed. More particularly, the forfaiter will need to be able to check the signatures of company officers endorsing the promissory notes or bills of exchange over to him.
3. *Who is the importer and in what country is he situated?* Not only is it important to establish the credibility of the underlying trade contract, but, without knowing who the importer is, the forfaiter will be unable to check the signatures of company officers signing promissory notes or their acceptance of bills of exchange which will be at the heart of the validity of those documents. Similarly, they may not be valid if drawn up in a manner not conforming with the importing country's laws or exchange control regulations.
4. *Who is the guarantor and in what country is he situated?*
5. *What is the form of the debt to be forfaited – bills, notes, etc.?*
6. *What is the form of the security to be offered?* Will it be an aval or a guarantee, etc.? (See Chapter 4 for a discussion of their relative merits.)
7. *In what amounts and at what dates do the bills or notes mature?*
8. *What sort of goods are to be exported?* With this question, the forfaiter is again seeking to satisfy himself as to the credibility of the business. He also wants to be sure that the goods are of a nature that he is happy to finance – for example, armaments are not universally popular!
9. *When will the goods be delivered?* This is likely to be very close to the date when finance will be provided. The important point is that the guarantor is unlikely to effect the aval or guarantee until delivery has taken place.
10. *When will the documents to be discounted arrive?* Until the forfaiter has the documents in his hands, he cannot check them and thus is unlikely to discount them, although discounting does sometimes take place

before this but 'under reserve' (see Chapter 4 for an explanation of this term).

11. *What licences and authorisations are needed to deliver the goods?* The forfaiter has a responsibility to ensure that there is no obvious impediment to the performance of the contract he is financing. Delays can cost money and entail embarrassment to all the parties involved.

12. *What is the 'domicile' of payment, that is, where will repayment be made to the forfaiter?* This question is important because payment to overseas banks can result in delays in the transfer of funds and such potential delays need to be allowed for (probably via a 'grace period', as explained in Chapter 5) in the discount that the forfaiter calculates when he buys the bills or notes. There is also, of course, the possibility that the authorities in a foreign country will freeze the funds and this possibility will influence the discount rate the forfaiter seeks or even determine whether or not he accepts the transaction.

These questions answered, what happens next?

Forfaiter's credit analysis

Most à forfait companies are either banks themselves or closely connected with banks. Credit analysis is therefore an integral part of their operations. There are four potential credit risks that need to be evaluated – the sovereign risk, the guarantor risk, the customer (exporter) risk and the importer risk. All these are considered in Chapter 8. Here, it is necessary only to note that the forfaiter will want to satisfy himself on the following points.

1. Does he have room, within the country limits on his portfolio, for the sovereign risk involved?
2. What is his evaluation of the credit-worthiness of the guarantor?
3. Does the proposed underlying commercial transaction sound a reasonable business proposition?
4. Has he any negative information about the competence, credibility or credit-worthiness of either the exporter or the importer?
5. Can he sell the paper at an acceptable price?

Because of the overriding importance of the bank guarantee or aval, he is unlikely to perform a full credit analysis of the exporter or the importer but will probably undertake a review, sufficient to establish the fourth point above, in respect of them. Since the guarantor is likely to be a bank or state institution, any banker providing forfaiting services should be able to establish his bona fides quickly. As a result, the forfaiter will be able to determine quickly whether or not he wishes to quote on the deal: indeed, forfaiters pride themselves that one of the hallmarks of their business is the ability to give an indication of their attitude to a proposed deal and also of the discount rate they are likely to want within hours of the initial approach, if not immediatley.

This chapter does not deal with the considerations which will determine the discount rate that the forfaiter seeks (see Chapter 5). However, it must be emphasised that, assuming he wishes to purchase the proposed bills or notes, he will, at this stage, only provide an indication of the discount rate he wants: he has made no commitments.

Option period and commitment period

If the quotation is acceptable to the exporter, he will wish to draw up his tender with the security of a definite finance cost from the forfaiter, who will therefore be asked to give a firm quotation. Since a considerable time may elapse between the submission of the tender and the shipment of the goods involved, there is a risk to the forfaiter that interest or currency rates may move substantially against him before he actually purchases the bills or notes. This period of risk can be split into two.

First, there is the period between the submission of his tender and its acceptance by the importer. Naturally, there is no certainty that the transaction will eventually take place and therefore the exporter can only be granted an option to accept the finance during this period. If this option period does not exceed 48 hours, the forfaiter will probably accept the inherent risks without charge: for a period in excess of 48 hours, he will levy a fee (see Chapter 5) and is, in any event, unlikely to grant an option period of longer than one month, though periods of two or three months are not unknown. In times of very volatile interest or currency rates, of course, no option period may be granted.

Second, there is the period between the acceptance of the tender and the delivery of the goods. During this period, which can be as long as 12 months, both forfaiter and exporter are committed to the financing deal: neither party would permit the other to walk away from it without meeting all the associated costs, including, in the one case, the costs to the exporter of arranging alternative and perhaps more expensive financing and, in the other, the costs to the forfaiter of any expensive funding commitments he has entered into in order to finance his purchase of the bills or notes. However, despite the symmetry of these commitments, the forfaiter will still levy a commitment fee (see Chapter 5) because his commitment blocks his capacity to take other, possibly more profitable, deals on to his books and he may well be unable to obtain commitments for his future funding requirements to hedge adverse interest-rate or currency movements.

Documentary requirements

Upon granting an option or entering into a commitment, whichever is appropriate to the particular circumstances of the transaction, the forfaiter will have sent an offer document, a telex to be confirmed in writing or a letter, to the exporter, setting out the proposed transaction. An example is shown in Appendix I.

In drawing up this document, the forfaiter will exhibit his professional expertise as he will need to outline any particular items (authorisations, permits, import licences, exchange control approvals, evidence of payment of stamp duties) of which he will need sight before discounting the bills or notes. Similarly, he will need to indicate any particular form that legal requirements in the countries involved impose upon the bills of exchange or promissory notes themselves. Some of these requirements may strike (see Chapter 4) at the very validity of the notes themselves and thus at the forfaiter's security while others may merely eliminate delays in the discounting date, but the forfaiter should pre-empt difficulties of any sort: a knowledge of the needs, country by country, is a vital part of his job.

It hardly needs stressing, too, that the forfaiter is committing himself now to using his funds in the future and that he therefore has an interest in ensuring, as far as he can, that the underlying trade will take place. The questions he originally asked concerning the type of goods to be exported and the name of the importer, and his consideration of the credit-worthiness of the importer, of the reasonableness of the anticipated transaction and of the ability of the exporter to deliver the right goods at the right time, are all aimed, in part, at providing this assurance.

Many of the documents requested by the forfaiter can be obtained before delivery of the goods. The forfaiter can then check them before the discounting date arrives. Naturally, anything that can be done to hasten the completion of formalities, thereby enabling discounting to be completed at the earliest possible opportunity, assists both the exporter and the forfaiter.

Lodging of avalised documents before delivery of goods

Once he has accepted the offer from the forfaiter, the exporter must arrange for his customer to prepare a series of bills of exchange or to sign acceptance of a series of promissory notes, whichever has been agreed. At this stage, too, he will arrange, probably via his own bank, for the avalising or guaranteeing bank to add its aval to the bills or notes or to prepare a separate letter of guarantee. The exporter will also endorse the bills or notes to the forfaiter 'without recourse'. Note, therefore, that everything is now set to enable discounting to take place even though the goods have yet to be shipped – indeed they may not even have been manufactured. The only missing links are the evidence of shipment which the forfaiter will want to see and, stemming from this, the issue dates of the bills or notes and their dates of maturity.

The blank bills or notes can now be lodged with a bank in the exporter's or forfaiter's country pending their completion as to dates. They will usually be accompanied by a letter of credit advising the bank that, when shipping documents are presented, these dates should be completed. Examples of a bill of exchange, a promissory note, avals and a letter of guarantee are shown in Appendix I.

Signatures

Only one more step needs to be performed by, or on behalf of, the forfaiter. This is the checking of the signatures on the bills or notes themselves and on the aval or letter of guarantee. A forfaiter prefers that this be arranged by the exporter's bank and that he receives the following type of confirmation: 'We confirm the authenticity of the signatures by .... and that these persons are authorised to commit the Company.' Instead, however, he may obtain only the following limited type of confirmation: 'The signatures by .... compare favourably with the specimens on file.'

In this latter event, or if the exporter's bank is unable or is unwilling to perform this task, the forfaiter is likely to confirm the signatures himself directly with the exporter, importer and guarantor.

Cash payment for the bills or notes

Once the shipping documents are to hand, the exporter will take them to the bank where the blank documents are lodged. The relevant dates will be inserted. The issue date will generally be the shipment date, the date of the bill of lading or a given number of days after the date of the bill of lading, depending upon the provisions of the letter of credit. The issue date will determine the maturity dates of the bills or notes.

Now that the documents are complete, the exporter can take them straight to the forfaiter, who will discount them immediately in accordance with the terms of his original offer. Having shipped the goods perhaps only the day before, the exporter has already received payment and has no further risk in connection with the transaction. Forfaiters maintain that the safety and speed of this form of finance are two of its principal attractions.

The forfaiter will provide the exporter with a discount statement indicating the discounted value of each of the bills or notes he is purchasing. The transaction is complete and the forfaiter has acquired a bank or state-guaranteed asset for his balance sheet or, unless the exporter has indicated that he does not wish it to happen, to trade in the secondary market. (The accounting and tax treatment of à forfait paper are considered in Chapter 9 and the secondary market and limitations upon trading à forfait paper were discussed in Chapter 1.)

In addition, the forfaiter may, at this point, write to the guarantor both as a matter of courtesy and, more specifically, to confirm the amounts, currency and maturity dates of the bills or notes involved. This latter point is, again, precautionary against delays and misunderstandings rather than mandatory.

Settlement

No further action need be taken in respect of the bills or notes bought until the date on which the first in the series matures. Shortly before maturity, the forfaiter will send the relevant bill or note to the avalising or guaranteeing institution for payment. Naturally, this, technically, represents a risk since there is always the danger of misappropriation by the guarantor. This can be overcome by using a third party to act as collection agent which also has the benefit of facilitating any protest against non-payment by the guarantor. Apart from the additional costs involved, however, this is normally regarded as unnecessary because no forfaiter would purchase paper backed by a guarantor he did not trust.

Failure to settle

The aval or guarantee will always be an absolute obligation and payment must be made immediately upon the maturity date. From time to time, legal disputes will arise between an exporter and importer but it is extremely rare for settlement of such an obligation to be delayed provided that the precautions outlined above have been taken by the forfaiter and the bill or note has been validly prepared, validly guaranteed or avalised and validly presented for payment, unless that delay is caused by supervening political or state reasons such as the lack of availability of the currency to pay. The forfaiter cannot avoid such a sovereign risk, but experience in recent years has shown that the absolute nature of the obligation has tended to mean that countries meeting such difficulties try to pay forfaited paper, with interest for late payment, at the earliest opportunity and, if possible, without any attempt at rescheduling the debt.

Should the obligation be dishonoured by the guarantor, however, the forfaiter must be prepared to lodge a legal protest. Because the obligation is absolute and failure to meet it highly damaging to the guarantor's reputation, a hint at legal action will probably be enough to expedite payment. If not, the exporter must be informed immediately of the difficulty, not only because he may be able to shed light on the cause, but because, as explained in Chapter 4, the forfaiter may have an action against him in certain circumstances. As to the legal action itself, the first question is likely to be the appropriate legal authority with whom to lodge the protest and the forfaiter's lawyers will need to establish this speedily so that the matter can be resolved as quickly and cheaply as possible.

Acceleration

One other point needs to be borne in mind in considering default by the guarantor. If this happens, it will occur when a particular bill or note is presented for payment. There may, of course, be several other bills or notes which were the subject of the forfaiting transaction but which have yet to mature. As stated in Chapter 2, payment of these remaining documents cannot be accelerated so that the forfaiter will never be in a position to call a default before their maturity. There is, therefore, a fundamental difference in this regard between à forfait financing and conventional lending where the loan agreements normally incorporate clauses whereby the lender can accelerate repayment once he has reason to suppose that the borrower will be unable to meet his obligations in the future.

Although this may seem, to a prudent banker, an important disadvantage of forfaiting, he must always remember that the avals or guarantees will have been provided, in most cases, by banks or state institutions so that the risks of non-payment are generally only sovereign ones. In similar circumstances in conventional lending, a sovereign risk may well not be overcome by calling an early default anyway.

4

Some technical aspects of à forfait finance

Hitherto, this book has been concerned to outline the essential theory of à forfait finance, the nature and development of the à forfait market, the characteristics of an à forfait transaction and the process by which an à forfait transaction is initiated and carried through to eventual payment of the forfaited debt obligations. If there has been one principal point to grasp, it is the simplicity of forfaiting: its comparison in Chapter 2 with other available forms of medium-term trade credit should have emphasised this.

Chapter 2 also examined the merits and demerits of forfaiting from the standpoint of the various parties to an à forfait transaction. In this chapter it is necessary to outline certain specific technicalities of forfaiting which, while affecting neither the simplicity nor the fundamental advantages and disadvantages of this form of finance, are significant to the forfaiter in fulfilling his function. Specifically, are there reasons for a forfaiter to favour a promissory note over a bill of exchange? What forms of security should he seek? Why is the nature of the transaction underlying a forfaiting deal important?

Are there differences between the responsibilities of a primary and a secondary forfaiter? Is conditional purchase, or 'purchase under reserve', necessary and should it be limited? What limitations does the 'without recourse' clause have? What problems are there in determining the jurisdiction and proper law applicable to any particular transaction?

In so far as the answers to these questions imply that the forfaiter should require certain specific forms of documentation, they may be unrealistic, since the practical reality of most à forfait transactions is that the forfaiter is often involved at too late a stage in the negotiations between the exporter, importer and guarantor to influence the documentation, particularly where those parties to the deal are already experienced in forfaiting. However, any forfaiter will need to be aware of the points below to protect himself and to conduct his business efficiently.

Technical difference between a bill of exchange and a promissory note

In Chapter 1, forfaiting is defined as the purchase, without recourse to any previous holder of the instruments, of debt instruments due to mature in the future and arising from the provision of goods and services. As stated, although there are several forms which such debt instruments might take, they are most likely to be either bills of exchange or promissory notes. These two instruments differ fundamentally from one another in that the former is drawn on the obligor by the beneficiary and accepted by the obligor, while the latter is issued by the obligor in favour of the beneficiary. This difference does not of itself render one preferable to the other in the eyes of the forfaiter since, provided that he can purchase a 'clean' obligation which gives him an absolute right to repayment irrespective of disputes arising between the exporter and the importer in respect of the underlying trade transaction, either instrument is simple to use and readily transferable.

However, there is a further distinction between these two forms of obligation which arises from the process of transfer from the beneficiary, the exporter, to the forfaiter. Both are transferred, or transmitted, by endorsement. This simple process, merely evidenced by the signature of the beneficiary on the bill or note, is accompanied by the use of the words 'without recourse' in the endorsement. The intention of the endorser in doing this is, of course, to free himself from any responsibilities in respect of the obligation: one of the cardinal principles of forfaiting, after all, is the assumption of all repayment risks by the forfaiter. If he did not use these words, or others to the same effect, the endorser would certainly remain liable as a guarantor of the obligation.

Article 9 of the International Convention for Commercial Bills established by the Geneva Conference of 1930 expressly states that 'the drawer [of a bill of exchange] guarantees both acceptance and payment. He may release himself from guaranteeing acceptance, but any stipulation by which he releases himself from the guarantee of payment is deemed to be not written.' Thus, the drawer of a bill of exchange, the exporter, may not be liable as its endorser but will always be liable as its drawer. This article does not apply to promissory notes. Indeed, under the terms of the convention, the endorser of a promissory note has the legal right to free himself of any liability by the use of a 'without recourse' clause in his endorsement.

This legal difference has the unsurprising consequence that a number of exporters favour promissory notes over bills of exchange as payment instruments. However, its practical significance should not be overemphasised since the forfaiter will always be prepared to give the exporter a written undertaking to the effect that he will not take any action against him in the event of non-payment of a bill of exchange that he has purchased, irrespective of his strict legal right to do so. In many countries, such a declaration by the forfaiter is legally enforceable by the exporter under the laws of contracts. Even in countries where this is not the case, it is virtually inconceivable that any respectable forfaiter would dishonour it. It does emphasise, though, the importance to the exporter of ensuring that he deals only with a reputable forfaiter. As a final point on this subject, it must be said that forfaiters generally find promissory notes and bills of exchange equally common in their business despite the legal distinctions.

Comparison of different forms of security

When a forfaiter purchases a series of notes or bills, he obviously wants the risks he is taking on to be in a form which he can easily assess. He can obtain information about the political and transfer risks associated with the debtor's country either from experience or from his company's credit analysts. His expertise will enable him to take a view on the interest-rate risks. However, one risk he cannot be expected to assess in every case is the ability of the importer to repay the notes or bills when they are due.

For this reason, the forfaiter usually requires that the paper he purchases be secured by a form of bank or state guarantee. He cannot possibly know each buyer but, as a banker, he certainly is in a position to know many other banks and will be able to indicate to the exporter those guarantors acceptable to him. In practice, there are three forms which such guarantees can take – the aval, the letter of guarantee and, more rarely, the burgschaft.

Aval

The aval comes from continental law, the *Code Napoléon*. Besides an actual signature, an aval involves writing on the promissory note or the bill of exchange the words 'per aval' and is completed by, in the case of a bill of exchange, the name of the person on whose behalf the aval is given. The avalist takes the place, in law, of the person who has committed himself in the promissory note or bill of exchange. So, when a bank gives its aval, it becomes the debtor as far as the forfaiter is concerned. Apart from the legal inevitability of the aval, it has the advantage of being inseparable from the instrument. It is thus a very simple and very clear undertaking and, very important, it remains an abstract obligation, that is, it is not dependent upon the performance of the underlying trade contract. Its transferability, therefore, does not give rise to the many problems, questions and complications to be found with independent guarantees issued on a separate document.

Incidentally, the aval is not legally recognised in every country where forfaiting is practised. For example, it is unknown to English law. Nevertheless, since an aval is an endorsement of a bill or note, it is probable that a signatory of an aval would have the same practical legal obligations in the United Kingdom as he would have in countries where avals are legally known. However, it has not been conclusively decided that an aval and an endorsement have the same effect; and, if they have, it must be remembered that, under English law, forgery of an endorsement breaks the chain of liability whereas the Geneva Convention, to which the United Kingdom was not a signatory, expressly provides that forgery of an aval will not affect liability. Note, though, that forfaiters, even in the United Kingdom, tend to favour an aval over a separate guarantee.

Examples of avals on a promissory note and on a bill of exchange are shown in Appendix I.

Letter of guarantee

There are occasions, however, when the various parties to a forfaiting transaction wish to express choices as to the jurisdiction or proper law to which it is to be subject or wish to clarify certain rights and responsibilities attached to it. In addition, in certain countries an aval may have an ambiguous or indeterminate legal status. In such circumstances, the debtor, guarantor or forfaiter might conclude that the additional documentation required tends to imply that a letter of guarantee rather than an aval be used.

A letter of guarantee is merely a separate document in which the guarantor commits himself to pay a series of notes or bills on their respective due dates. Like the aval, a guarantee must be abstract and, therefore, make no conditional reference to an underlying commercial contract. This is, as already stated, to avoid a situation whereby a forfaiter, having paid the exporter without the possibility of recourse, suddenly finds that payment is withheld by the importer because of an alleged defect in the goods. The dispute involves only the importer and exporter as in a cash transaction and does not affect the financing institution.

In respect of the wording of the guarantee, the important point is that there is as yet no internationally recognised standard form. A careful forfaiter will, however, at least make sure that there are some provisions in the guarantee itself expressing clearly that it is fully transferable, assignable, divisible and unconditional, that the guarantor is a primary debtor as far as the purchaser is concerned and that, consequently, he cannot resort to the type of defences that the acceptor of the bills might wish to raise and which normally would relate to the underlying transaction.

Although perfectly satisfactory for the purpose of forfaiting, letters of guarantee involve more work for the forfaiter than avals. They are usually nominative documents, that is, issued in favour of the exporter, who must therefore issue a letter of assignment to the forfaiter. At the same time, it is prudent for the forfaiter to advise the guaranteeing bank of his beneficial interest in the guarantee. However, the only real drawback with a letter of guarantee becomes significant when the forfaiter wishes to sell a bill or note from the series to another party. In such cases, the investor will have beneficial ownership of that bill or note, but the forfaiter will be unable to give up the guarantee as it still covers the others in the series. In other words, the guarantee is, whatever its wording, in practice not divisible.

An example of a letter of guarantee is shown in Appendix I.

Burgschaft

The third and final form of bank guarantee found in forfaiting is the burgschaft – a word with no appropriate direct English translation. Burgschafts are the least common of the three forms of security and are usually used only by East Germany. It is a declaration of liability which is conditional on the legality of the underlying contract. This, of course, means that it cannot be accepted by a forfaiter until he has satisfied himself that the contract has been satisfactorily completed. In practice, he must obtain from the guarantor confirmation of the receipt of the goods in good order. There must also be no counter-claims outstanding and no changes in the amounts due and dates at which they are due. The guarantor must declare his agreement with any transfer of the burgschaft and that he is unconditionally and irrevocably committed by it. All these requirements effectively reduce the burgschaft to a straightforward unconditional, irrevocable letter of guarantee.

Specifying the nature of the underlying transaction – financial or trade-backed

The first concern to a forfaiter when asked to quote on any proposed à forfait transaction is the nature of the underlying trade. Is the paper trade-backed or does it support a financial transaction? Trade-backed paper here means paper issued to pay for goods; financial paper means paper issued in order to borrow funds which the borrower may then use as he wishes. It must be said that the distinction does tend to become blurred. For instance, some bills are issued to raise funds which are then immediately applied in the purchase of goods. Such bills obviously have elements of both financial and trade-backed paper, especially if the purchase of goods transaction is lined up before the bills are actually issued and the funds raised. At the end of the day, however, forfaiters do recognise a distinction between trade-backed paper and financial paper. Consequently, it is important to establish which type of paper is involved at the outset of any forfaiting transaction. There are two reasons for this.

First, some people dealing in the à forfait market are unwilling to purchase financial as opposed to trade-backed paper. Various different explanations are given for this unwillingness. Some regard obtaining finance in this way on the à forfait market as an expensive method of borrowing and feel that any borrower who needs to resort to this method of raising funds must be financially weak: in fact, however, very reputable people do borrow in this fashion. Others seem to take comfort from the fact that, in a trade-backed transaction, the purchaser will have the goods from which to produce profits so that they are some form of tangible 'security' in the commercial rather than the legal sense. Others regard financial paper with some disfavour since goods are less likely to be misappropriated than money and there have been instances to justify such caution.

Second, even those who are willing to buy financial paper want to know which type of paper they are dealing with, since it may affect their assessment of the credit risk and the sort of questions they ask. For instance, since money is easier to steal than merchandise, the seller of financial paper will normally be asked whether the borrower has actually received the funds.

Since most of the paper dealt in on the à forfait market is trade-backed, the market usually deals on the basis that any paper offered for sale on the primary or secondary à forfait markets is implicitly trade-backed paper unless the contrary is expressly stated by the seller. Of course, unless the express statement is in writing, this is a fruitful source of dispute.

The difference between the two types of paper is regarded by the market as so fundamental that any secondary purchaser who mistakenly buys financial paper in the absence of any such express statement may feel entitled to require the seller to take it back from him. Whether such an entitlement exists in law even when nothing has been specified in writing has never been properly tested, though it was claimed in the second case outlined in Chapter 10.

As a precaution, even when dealing with trade-backed bills, a primary or secondary forfaiter is well advised to specify this in writing (preferably before there is a contractual commitment but at least in the confirmatory documentation). As a secondary but related point, a forfaiter should also specify the nature of the goods being dealt with in the transaction. This should help to avoid any disputes between purchaser and seller if the purchaser thinks, for example, that the bills emanate from a transaction about cranes whereas in fact they emanate from a transaction about excavators.

In short, it is generally sensible to have a written statement about the subject matter of the underlying transaction in any offer telex: indeed, scope for dispute as to the terms agreed is much reduced if there is one document setting them all out. However, it is fair to add that the documents supporting an à forfait transaction are often less specific about the details of the underlying business than are here suggested as prudent.

The role of the primary forfaiter

In Chapter 1, the evolution of the primary and secondary à forfait markets is described. This section considers why the distinction between the primary market and the secondary market is important in terms of the obligations of the forfaiter.

It is the duty of each seller in the à forfait market, whether primary or secondary, to sell a valid claim relating to a bona fide transaction. That is to say that, if any purchaser finds himself with paper which does not constitute a valid claim against the importer or a guarantee that does not constitute a valid claim against the guarantor, he can bring an action against his seller. As explained later in this chapter, in such circumstances even a 'without recourse' clause might not prevent this.

The distinction between the primary and the secondary market, however, is crucial, because, although the point has not been legally determined, the market in which one is dealing probably affects the obligations of the purchaser rather than those of the seller. In other words, the purchaser from the exporter – here referred to as the primary forfaiter – is probably obliged to carry out the necessary checks to ensure that the paper he will subsequently sell on the à forfait market does constitute a valid claim relating to a bona fide transaction. The purchaser in the secondary market, on the other hand, may not have such obligations. If this is a correct analysis of the responsibilities in the market, any secondary purchaser could always pass liability on to the seller to him and hence there would be a chain of liability all the way up to the primary forfaiter. Indeed, the liability could be passed up to the exporter since he has the same obligation to sell a valid claim relating to a bona fide transaction but this is of no practical benefit to secondary forfaiters when the exporter is bankrupt, as in the first case in Chapter 10, or simply does not exist, as in the second case in Chapter 10.

There are three obvious reasons why the obligation to check that there is a valid claim relating to a bona fide transaction rests with the primary forfaiter. In the first place, he will have been directly involved with the exporter in buying the paper and will have had every opportunity to check out the bona fides of the exporter, to enquire into the contractual documentation and otherwise look into the transaction giving rise to the issue of the paper. In practice, the exporter will often be his customer. To have subsequent purchasers in the à forfait market also do this checking would lead to needless duplication and delay. Furthermore, it would be impracticable.

In any given transaction in the secondary market, any seller is likely to approach a number of potential purchasers who the seller thinks will be interested in the transaction. The majority of these are unlikely to purchase the paper. However, if all those potential purchasers have to check into the transaction in detail, the basic contractual documentation underlying the notes would probably need to go to many banks in different places. The time involved in photocopying the documents and sending them around the world would make transactions in the market much slower. As the market believes one of its main attractions is the speed of its response, this is important.

Second, a bank introducing an à forfait transaction to a secondary forfaiter frequently chooses not to disclose the identity of the exporter until after the transaction is concluded. Apart from anything else, this is often done to prevent any offerees of the paper from getting in touch directly with the exporter and trying to cut out the primary forfaiter. Third, a banker's general duties of confidentiality will normally mean that he is not at liberty to distribute documents relating to the underlying transaction around the market at large. These last two limitations prevent any secondary purchaser of bills from going directly to the exporter, which is the obvious method of checking it since he could look at the exporter's underlying contractual documentation.

For these practical reasons, it seems eminently sensible that it should be the clear responsibility of the primary forfaiter to carry out these checks and to be the party ultimately responsible if the paper that is sold in the à forfait market does not emanate from a bona fide transaction giving rise to a valid claim. These practical reasons are probably more important than the legal ones because they reflect the commercial reality of transactions on the à forfait market. It is, however, worth while to consider the legal reasoning.

The legal reason why the primary forfaiter should be liable if paper does not satisfy these requirements is that he has failed to sell what he has agreed to sell, that is, a valid bill validly guaranteed or avalised. In other words, an à forfait transaction is like an ordinary sale of goods and, if the bills are not true bills, it is as if the primary forfaiter, having agreed to sell a horse, has sold a cow. There is no legal reason why the market should not change the burden of responsibility to the purchaser and work on the basis of *caveat emptor*. However, for the practical reasons set out above, the purchaser cannot be expected to carry out proper checks and must therefore rely on the seller.

Given this duty, it must rest with the primary forfaiter to decide what sort of checks he wants to do. It is not up to the market to dictate how the primary forfaiter is to satisfy himself that he is selling a valid claim coming from a bona fide transaction. He must satisfy himself as he thinks fit but recognising that (if the above principles are correct) he will be liable if he carries out no checks or inadequate ones. In practice, obviously, the amount of checking the primary forfaiter carries out in a transaction will depend upon various factors such as his degree of involvement with the underlying transaction, his own knowledge of the exporter and the exporter's status.

Another area where the primary forfaiter may have very specific obligations not shared by secondary market purchasers is in the area of checking the security, that is, the guarantee or aval. Again, there is some uncertainty, to resolve which there have been, to date, no legal decisions, as to whether any purchaser of the paper is regarded as being under an obligation to contact the guarantor to ascertain that the guarantee is in order and still effective; or whether this is merely prudent; or whether this is an unnecessary duplication of work.

It would certainly lead to unnecessary duplication of work for each and every purchaser of bills arising from the transaction to get in touch with the guarantor. To avoid this, one of the obligations of the primary forfaiter alone may be to obtain written confirmation from the guarantor that the guarantee is unconditionally in force because his access to information and documents gives him, as noted earlier, a unique practical opportunity to fulfil this responsibility. Copies of any written confirmation should be passed on to purchasers who should not be regarded as being under any obligation to get in touch with the guarantor, though of course they may do so if they wish.

It is probably not necessary that the confirmation from the guarantor that the guarantee is still in order should contain an undertaking that the guarantor will notify immediately whomsoever has obtained the confirmation if anything goes wrong: such evidence as does exist on the subject shows that a guarantor or, at least, a guaranteeing bank would owe a duty in accordance with normal banking practice to notify the person to whom the confirmation had been given if any problems should come to its notice. The primary forfaiter can therefore offer the protection to his purchaser that he has not heard anything from the guarantor about the standing of the guarantee and this protection can then be offered on down the line.

There may, of course, be occasions on which the primary forfaiter wants to opt out of his obligations. This may happen, for example, when a financier who would otherwise be the primary forfaiter says to someone else who deals in the market that he has a customer who is an exporter but he does not wish to buy paper from him. If the financier is in direct touch with the ultimate forfaiter, he is, in these circumstances, merely acting as a broker and clearly undertaking no responsibilities. The market has no specific form of words which a broker can use nor a requirement that the broker pass on specific information such as the name of the exporter, his address, telephone and telex number. For his own protection, however, the broker must make his status clear in writing so that he cannot be ascribed the responsibilities of the primary forfaiter, passing them on instead directly to the true forfaiter.

Reserves

It is not uncommon for a forfaiter to purchase a debt obligation, particularly in the secondary market, with a proviso. In such circumstances, he is said to purchase 'under reserve', which simply means that he is reserving his right to rescind his purchase if certain conditions are not met. For example, he may impose a reserve to the effect that he must be allowed to examine the documentation in the transaction and find it satisfactory or that the seller of the bill must obtain confirmation from the guarantor that he will pay direct to the purchaser or that the seller must satisfy himself that the obligations being sold are valid and legally binding.

In practical terms, one can see that, where a purchaser is buying without even seeing the documents, he will feel strongly tempted to make the transaction conditional upon his satisfactory examination of them. Again, given the significance of both a guarantor's responsibilities and the form of the obligations themselves, a reserve relating to the willingness of the guarantor to pay the purchaser or to the validity of the obligations may seem important. However, in reality, there is usually no genuine necessity to impose reserves.

For example, if the primary forfaiter is under an obligation to sell a valid claim relating to a bona fide transaction, there is no real need to impose a reserve relating to satisfactory examination of the documentation since, if there is no valid claim relating to a bona fide transaction, the primary forfaiter is anyhow liable notwithstanding any 'non-recourse' clause. (This limitation of the 'non-recourse' clause is explored more fully below.) However, if such a reserve is imposed, it should contain a term expressed or implied that, unless the purchaser objects within seven days of receipt of the documents, he is deemed to be satisfied. By the same token, a reserve requiring that the seller provide valid and legally binding obligations is unnecessary, since it merely restates a duty he has anyway.

Again, as far as the concurrence of the guarantor to payment details is concerned, a confirmatory letter appropriately worded and obtained as suggested in the previous section should remove any necessity for a reserve. (However, a buyer may well want to introduce some form of condition about withholding tax to ensure that he will receive the full amount of the face value of the bill together with interest at the rate expressed.) If, in practice, a purchaser wants some comfort directly from the guarantor, he should indicate this at the time of his acceptance of the offer and a time should then be agreed beyond which failure to obtain the necessary confirmation will mean that the transaction is deemed to be null and void unless subsequently agreed otherwise.

As a general point, any forfaiter must realise that the question of reserves is one of the most difficult areas in law and thus their imposition needs to be carefully circumscribed. In English law, it is not possible to impose a reserve after the stage of the telexed acceptance of an offer. In any event, there should be a time clearly laid down in each transaction after which it would not be open to a purchaser to impose a reserve. One has only to look at the position of a secondary market purchaser further up the line who may not have imposed a reserve and finds himself faced with a reserve when he sells to realise the obvious sense in such a limitation.

The area of reserves is perhaps the one which can give rise to the greatest uncertainty in the operation of the market. Eventually, the market may lay down clear rules as to what sort of reserves can be imposed and when they can be imposed, bearing in mind the obligations which lie upon the seller of a bill by which the purchaser can have recourse to the seller even if no reserve is imposed. No such rules exist at present.

Limitations of the 'without recourse' clause

It is necessary to look at the meaning of the words 'without recourse' and how far these absolve the seller of responsibility. These words are a term of the contract between the seller of a bill or note and the purchaser. A lawyer therefore tends to say that it is irrelevant that the subject matter of the contract is, for example, bills of exchange and looks at the words as a standard form of exclusion clause applied to a contract for sale. In the case of an à forfait transaction, it merely happens to be a contract for sale of debt obligations though it could as well be for sale of cars. The meaning of the words has been much canvassed, since, if they were wide enough to absolve the seller of a bill or note of all liability whatever had gone wrong, its purchaser would be left to suffer any loss in the event of any default in repayment.

The fact that none of the liability in the second case outlined in Chapter 10 fell upon those who had purchased in the secondary market shows fairly clearly that the parties in that case did not consider the words 'without recourse' could be as widely construed as this. The evidence gathered from everywhere else also leads to this conclusion. The obligation of the forfaiter and, indeed, of the exporter is, as already stated, to sell bills constituting a valid claim relating to a bona fide transaction and nobody appears to regard the words 'without recourse' as in any way qualifying or restricting this obligation.

The words 'without recourse' would not therefore exclude liability for misrepresentation if, for instance, the seller describes the paper as being trade-backed when it is financial paper; neither would they exclude liability if there is some fundamental defect in the transaction with the result that the bills are not true bills; neither would they if some other problem arises.

What the words do, in the opinion of everyone, is to exclude any liability on the drawer of the bill and any seller of the bill if the bill is not met because the acceptor and/or guarantor are insolvent and cannot pay or if payment of the bills is prevented by, for example, exchange control restrictions, change of Government, war, supervening governmental action, etc. 'Without recourse' means that any purchaser takes on the credit risk that the acceptor and guarantor may not pay and also the risk that *force majeure* may prevent payment.

It may be something of an over-simplification, but it seems fair to say that, provided that the bill may be validly sued on and a valid judgement obtained at the time of the sale of the bill, the seller will have complied with his obligations. 'Without recourse' protects the seller if a judgement properly obtained cannot be enforced or executed but not if, at the day of sale, a judgement could not be obtained. The words may also protect the seller if, when a purchaser sues the importer on the bills, the courts in the importer's country do not recognise the principle of the abstract nature of bills. If this is correct and the importer's domestic courts take the view that defect in the goods goes to the validity of the bills themselves, 'without recourse' would absolve the seller of liability.

There appears to be some uncertainty as to whether or not the words 'without recourse' protect the seller of the bill if the bills of exchange are defective because they did not comply with the requirements of the proper law of the bills and were therefore formally invalid, for example, if the law governing the bills of exchange requires them to be drawn on bright green paper but they have not been so drawn. Some seem to feel that the purchaser takes on the risk of formal invalidity while others do not. In terms of general principle, if the exporter or forfaiter sells a bill which is formally invalid, he has failed to comply with his legal obligations, that is, he has not sold what he has agreed to sell, a valid bill validly guaranteed or avalised.

In transactions between forfaiters, there is no reason in principle why the market should not say that the legal position is that, as regards formal invalidity, it is a question of *caveat emptor*. Even though a system of having responsibilities divided between the primary forfaiter and secondary forfaiters as to who is to ensure that bills are valid and true is inherently dangerous and would be a potential source of disputes, it is possible to draw a practical distinction between matters for which the primary forfaiter must in all fairness be responsible, namely matters relating to the transaction itself which cannot be in the knowledge of any subsequent buyer, and matters which can be left to the buyer to satisfy himself about by means of general enquiry, for example, matters such as the exchange control restrictions of the country from which the payment is to be made and withholding taxes. Provided a buyer knows which law governs the bills – and this may be something of a large proviso if he is unaware of the identity of the exporter and has not seen the bills – he can make independent checks as to whether or not the bills appear to have been validly drawn in a formal sense. Nevertheless, this may be difficult if he cannot make direct enquiries of the importer and exporter as to the precise circumstances in which the bills have been issued and delivered.

The market has not yet, however, adopted this approach. Therefore, in the absence of such further or express clarification of the responsibility of the buyer to ensure the formal validity of the bills, the balance of probability supports those who believe that this duty is the seller's to perform.

In short, as stated earlier, the primary forfaiter has duties which do not befall secondary market forfaiters and which he must fulfil in order to ensure that he is selling valid bills or notes, validly guaranteed or avalised and arising from a bona fide transaction: if the documents he is selling do not satisfy these conditions then he is unlikely to be able to rely on the 'without recourse' clause. By the same token, in such circumstances the exporter will not be able to rely on the 'without recourse' clause either.

Jurisdiction and proper law appropriate to an à forfait transaction

The first difficulty encountered when there is a problem relating to an à forfait transaction is the choice of jurisdiction, that is, the courts which will have the authority to hear the case. Because very little is committed to writing, typically there is no express clause in any forfaiting document on the submission of possible litigation to the courts of a particular jurisdiction. It is usually simply assumed that first jurisdiction is to be recognised by the courts of the place where the bill or note is payable and where it can be protested. One cannot exclude, however, the risk that a plaintiff might find it difficult to convince a court in the particular country that it has jurisdiction over a particular case. In the absence of an express choice by the parties, most courts would require some sort of connecting factor between the case and the country in which the action is brought. It is not enough, for instance under English law, that the plaintiff has a presence in England for him to be able to submit a case to the English courts. There is the additional requirement that a defendant has also some sort of presence or that the action is connected with the enforcement of a contract governed by English law or that the breach of the contract has occurred in England or that there are some other connections with England.

In cases where there is a separate guarantee instrument instead of an aval, the forfaiter can include in its wording a provision ordaining the jurisdiction to which it is to be subject, thereby removing this problem in respect of it. For that reason, although the aval is a simpler document than a letter of guarantee and has the advantages outlined earlier in this chapter, many lawyers would deem a letter of guarantee preferable. In addition, as also noted earlier, the aval is not legally recognised in certain countries, for example, the United Kingdom. However, in practice, the aval is the more commonly found form of security in the à forfait market, so that the difficulty usually remains.

Quite apart from the problem of jurisdiction, there is the problem of the proper law governing any à forfait transaction. When no specific provision pertaining to the law exists to govern the transaction, the bills or notes may be governed by one law, the guarantee by another and the sales of the bills or notes in the secondary market by yet a third law. In fact, things may well be more complex than this implies because determining which laws and how many govern the transaction may be very difficult. Furthermore, even if the applicable laws can be determined with certainty, the provisions of those particular laws might not themselves be crystal clear. Consequently, litigation might produce different results in different jurisdictions but, more likely, severe timing problems might arise: a litigant might therefore find himself liable without immediately being able to pass the liability on.

Indeed, problems do not necessarily disappear even when a particular jurisdiction and proper law are selected. For example, where English law governs a transaction, it is necessary to establish a party's ability to enter into that transaction by reference to his own domestic law. Similarly, whether or not a transaction is illegal will be dependent upon its place of performance even though it is subject to English law and is perfectly legal under English law.

Again, where a separate letter of guarantee is used, the inclusion of some wording making it clear that the guarantee, if not the entire transaction, is to be governed by a particular law is helpful since it is this law which will then determine the scope and extent of the obligations of the guarantor. This is a very important point since, in the absence of any such provision, unexpected problems might arise.

For instance, perhaps the law of the place where the debtor resides will govern the validity of the guarantee. This could raise a number of difficulties for the forfaiter or the purchasers of the paper in the secondary market since, for example, there might be a number of formal requirements to be complied with in the guarantor's country for the guarantee to be fully valid and binding. As an illustration, one can imagine that, under a particular system of law, a guarantee is deemed to be validly given only if issued on a particular type of paper or registered with a public registrar of one sort or another.

When no law governing the bills or notes has been stipulated, there are some general guidelines it is possible to state. It is the common rule that formal validity has to be decided under the provisions of the law of the place of issue. This is understood to be the place where a debt obligation was first delivered complete in form and not the place where it was signed. Here, again, one has to be very careful when dealing with bills of exchange or promissory notes inasmuch as a country which is not a member of the International Convention for Commercial Bills might have particular requirements regarding the form of a bill or note for it to be considered as valid under the law of that particular country.

With regard to the question of the power of a party to a bill or note to become such a party, the authority of the signatory is a matter to be decided by the laws of the place where the party is incorporated or established or where he is deemed to have his domicile. This is similar to the position of a signatory to a guarantee. It is a matter of very great practical importance since there are a number of countries in which foreign exchange control regulations make it illegal for a party residing in that particular country to borrow in foreign denominated notes or to sign bills of exchange or notes with foreign parties. In some jurisdictions, the consequence of the failure to obtain government consent could be such that a party to a transaction would be deemed not to have the proper authority to be a party to it so that, as a consequence, the bill or note or the guarantee would simply be deemed to be null and void and of no effect.

There is a further point arising from the question of applicable law. There are numerous requirements pertaining to the presentation of a bill or note for payment which is generally a necessary step in obtaining the right of recourse against its drawer and endorsers. It is, as a rule, the law of the place where it is dishonoured which will determine the scope of the duties of the holder of a bill or note with respect to the necessity of his notice of dishonour. Where the holder of a bill or note thinks that it will be dishonoured, it is not sufficient for him to refrain from presenting it for payment. The holder will be dispensed from the requirement to do so only in limited cases where such presentation cannot be reasonably expected, for example if the drawee is a fictitious person or where presentation is expressly or implicitly waived or for reasons of *force majeure*.

Whenever a bill or note is drawn in one country, accepted in a second, guaranteed in a third and payable in a fourth, the difficulties in the event of litigation do not stop with the determination of the proper jurisdiction or the proper law to be applied but extend to the series of other problems pertaining to the enforcement of the judgement itself if it should be sought in a country other than the place where it was rendered. There might be rules of procedure which make it difficult or expensive and there might be tax liabilities on the recovery of money by the creditor.

5

Costs of
à forfait finance

Costs to the importer

The only direct cost to the importer of the provision of à forfait finance is a guarantee fee. This will generally be a percentage of the face value of the bills or notes to be guaranteed or avalised. The percentage itself is a matter for negotiation between the importer and the guarantor.

In those instances where the forfaiter does not insist upon a guarantee, the forfaiter may himself require an equivalent fee, the percentage again open to negotiation, which reflects the additional risk which the forfaiter is therefore accepting.

The guarantee fee will generally be expressed as a percentage per annum of the average face value of the bills or notes outstanding during each year to final maturity, and will usually be payable each year in advance. Exceptionally, the fee may be calculated in the same way but be payable in a lump sum as soon as the guarantee or aval is signed. Occasionally, it may be calculated as a percentage per annum of the face value of each individual bill or note and be payable for each bill or note at its maturity.

Costs to the exporter

There are three elements in the costs which an exporter may bear when he arranges à forfait finance. These are the discount rate, or rate of interest, which the forfaiter will apply to the bills or notes when he purchases them, commitment fees and option fees.

Discount rate

The discount rate is, of course, a function of interest rates for the currency in which the bills or notes are denominated that prevail at the time the forfaiter commits himself to the deal. In general, the basis from which a forfaiter starts in determining the discount rate he requires is the market rate for funds over the average period to maturity of the bills or notes he is buying. In the case, for example, of a series of bills of equal face value denominated in US dollars and maturing in equal numbers at six-monthly intervals over five years, the first maturing six months hence, the average period to maturity is two and three-quarter years. The forfaiter will thus use prevailing US dollar interest rates for two and a half to three years' funds as his starting point.

He must then decide what premium over this basic rate he wants. The main component of this premium will reflect the risk he believes to be inherent in the deal. In general, he will not perceive this risk as arising from default by the guarantor as he will have accepted only a first-class guarantor in the first place. Despite all the cautionary suggestions and the tales of deals that went wrong which this book contains, very few à forfait deals have turned sour and fewer still have proved problematical because of a refusal to pay by the guarantor. In so far as repayment has been a problem, this has generally arisen from political difficulties or transfer difficulties arising from a lack of foreign exchange: in short, the major risk has been sovereign risk. Nevertheless, it is true that a forfaiter will attach a slightly smaller premium to a deal guaranteed by a state bank or a major international bank than to one whose guarantor is an ordinary commercial bank. This reflects, if anything, the greater clout that the first two classes of bank have in avoiding or circumventing political difficulties.

The principal risk, then, is sovereign risk. Different countries will mean different risk premiums at different times. While it is imprudent to be specific here, it is possible to say that the risk premium will vary between $\frac{1}{2}\%$ and 5% for most countries.

The next component in the premium recognises the fact that à forfait finance is fixed-rate finance. This should not be a significant amount as the forfaiter, in theory, has the opportunity to match his funding to the maturities of the bills or notes, thereby eliminating any exposure from interest-rate fluctuations. However, funds for exact matching over an extended period may not always be available at an acceptable interest rate, so that he may have to accept exposure for some time at least. More important, most forfaiters believe the fixed-rate nature of the finance to be one of its principal attractions and therefore see this component in the premium as reflecting that.

There is one other point, too, relating to this part of the premium. Where the bills or notes are denominated in a currency other than those commonly traded in the Euromarkets, it may be particularly difficult for the forfaiter to obtain matching funding. This increases his exposure to interest-rate movements unless he is able to fund in a different currency with spot and forward foreign exchange cover: in other words, he may choose to use a foreign exchange 'swap'. For example, he may be purchasing notes denominated in Spanish pesetas, half maturing one year hence and half two years hence. He chooses to fund the purchase in Deutschmarks and sells the Deutschmarks immediately ('spot') for Spanish pesetas which he uses to buy the paper. He simultaneously contracts to sell the Spanish pesetas he will receive 12 months hence and the ones due two years hence for Deutschmarks which he will use to repay his funding. Swaps have a cost and this part of the premium that the forfaiter charges the exporter will, in such a case, reflect that cost.

The third component of the premium will be set to cover the forfaiter's own management and administration expenses, as well as the profit which he hopes to make. In general, this adds about $\frac{1}{2}\%$ to the rate quoted. However, in determining this, the forfaiter will have regard to a number of questions.

First, how anxious is he to deal with this exporter? It hardly needs to be said that, if he sees the potential for much profitable future business, the forfaiter will be very careful to maximise his competitiveness. How keen is he to obtain more business anyhow? Forfaiting can be a way of building up a bank's assets quickly. If the forfaiter happens to want to increase the size of his balance sheet, he will offer finer rates than he would if already up to his funding limits.

Perhaps he has little room within his portfolio limits for more paper with the particular country risk he is being offered. Perhaps he is keen to build a relationship with the guarantor or, conversely, perhaps he already has enough exposure to that guarantor. Perhaps he knows that there are secondary forfaiters prepared to take paper with that country risk or that guarantor, and he knows he can sell the paper on to them at a particularly beneficial price. All these points will contribute to his decision as to the premium he wants.

Finally, he will consider interest-rate trends. Naturally, the basic interest rate that the forfaiter will have obtained from the market will reflect the market's perception of likely future movements. However, there is probably no financier alive who does not have his own view of them, even if that view is that it is impossible to say! This will colour his attitude to the prevailing rate, as it will, indeed, to the need to match his funding to the maturity dates of the bills or notes themselves. His perception of the trends may cause him to increase or reduce his required premium, but any such adjustment is likely to be only marginal.

One other point should be made in respect of the discount rate that the forfaiter will require. In general, paper immediately available will be discounted a slightly lower rates than paper which the forfaiter will not be able to buy for some months. In other words, where there is a period during which the forfaiter and exporter are committed to a future deal, the forfaiter will tend to ask for a higher premium over the relevant basic interest rate. Since, as explained in Chapter 3, neither party can renege on a deal during this period, it is difficult to see a logical reason for this, particularly since the forfaiter will certainly expect a commitment fee for this period to cover the opportunity costs that would arise if his commitment, in effect, precluded his acceptance of other, more profitable and/or immediately available business. However, this is a feature of the market.

Many forfaiters publish a list of rate indications each month. A specimen of a forfaiting rate indication sheet can be seen in Appendix II.

Commitment fees

The occasion for and justification of a commitment fee are explained in Chapter 3. The fee is normally quoted as a monthly or annual percentage of the face value of the bills or notes to be forfaited and is charged for the period between the date the commitment is agreed and the date the discounting takes place. It may be as low as $\frac{3}{4}\%$ per annum or as high as $1\frac{1}{2}\%$ per annum, but the most commonly quoted rate is 1 per mille per month – or 1.2% per annum. It is usually payable monthly in advance.

Option fees

Again, Chapter 3 explains the reason for an option fee and when it becomes chargeable. Unlike the commitment fee, an option fee is generally charged at a flat percentage of the face value of the bills or notes to be forfaited: it is not related to the length of the option period. Since an option period will rarely be permitted by the forfaiter to exceed three months, this means that the usual charge, $\frac{1}{8}\%$, is relatively high. This emphasises the fact that, during the option period, the forfaiter is carrying all the risks of the transaction without any certainty that it will eventually take place so that he is unable to enter into any commitment for funding to hedge the paper.

Grace period

There is one further point that needs to be mentioned in connection with the costs to the exporter. This is the 'grace period'.

It has been stated in this book, and indeed it seems obvious, that the amount of the discount charged by the forfaiter will be calculated by applying the interest rate he requires over the period from the date he purchases the paper to the dates the bills or notes are repaid. It is not, however, always reasonable to assume that the repayment dates are synonymous with the paper's maturity dates.

In theory, as implied in Chapter 3, they are. In practice, they often are not. The transfer of funds from the guarantor to the forfaiter may be delayed by the state bank in the guarantor's country while permission to effect the transfer is confirmed or obtained, or it may be delayed simply because of inefficiency on the part of the guarantor or his or the forfaiter's transfer agent, that is, the bank where the guarantor or the forfaiter holds the current accounts from or to which the funds are to be transferred. In many cases, such delays are not significant. However, any delay represents a loss of interest to the forfaiter: time costs money. Therefore, as a safeguard against such an eventuality, the forfaiter will often add a number of days, a 'grace period', to the period over which the discount is calculated. This may be only two or three days but, where the forfaiter has reason to expect a longer delay than this, usually because he or other forfaiters have bitter experience to justify it, it can be as much as 20 days or even more.

This, of course, can add a not insignificant amount to the exporter's discount costs. Similarly, when a primary forfaiter sells paper into the secondary à forfait market, he may find that a purchaser from him has a more pessimistic view of transfer delays than he had when buying the paper in the first place, and thus demands a longer grace period than he originally negotiated with the exporter. In this case, the price at which the primary forfaiter can sell may be considerably reduced. Not surprisingly, therefore, the length of the grace period can be hotly disputed between forfaiters or between an exporter and a forfaiter.

One means of resolving the problem involves the agreement between the parties in dispute that any delay over that assumed in the calculation of the price at the time of the sale of the paper will result in the payment of interest by the seller, in the one case the exporter, in the other the primary forfaiter, to the buyer, that is, the primary forfaiter or the secondary forfaiter. The rate of interest will generally be either that inherent in the agreed purchase price itself, in other words the rate used to calculate the discount, or the market rate at the time of the delay plus a fixed premium, for example LIBOR plus $\frac{1}{4}$%. Naturally, any interest received from the transfer agent or the guarantor in recognition of his responsibility for any delay will be deducted from any amount payable.

The corollary of such an agreement is the payment by the purchaser of interest, probably at one of the two rates just indicated, for any time by which repayment of the paper occurs earlier than the grace period assumed. However, while interest for a period of delay greater than that originally agreed in the sale contract is not uncommon between forfaiters, interest for earlier payment than anticipated is, and, in practice, it is virtually unheard of for a dispute as to the length of the grace period between an exporter and a forfaiter to result in an agreement for payment from one to the other in either eventuality. There are two reasons for the latter. First, the whole point of à forfait finance, from the exporter's standpoint, is that, once he has sold his debt obligation, the whole transaction is ended and no uncertainty exists as to the amount of money he can expect to receive. Second, the exporter generally concedes that the forfaiter is experienced in the matter of payment transfer and is unlikely to be capricious over such a comparatively minor matter. Therefore, if disagreement in this area persists, the deal simply does not get done.

Between forfaiters, however, disagreement may be deep: disagreement between experts often is. If so, there is one variation of the 'additional interest' approach mentioned above which may be adopted, although it must be emphasised that it is very seldom used as it is somewhat 'messy' and therefore forfaiters usually contrive to reach agreement without resorting to it. The price to be paid by the secondary forfaiter is calculated twice, once assuming the shorter grace period wanted by the primary forfaiter and once assuming the longer period the secondary forfaiter wants. The buyer will pay over the lower amount with the understanding that he will hold the difference between this and the higher amount in suspense until the paper is repaid. Interest will accrue on this sum, probably at the rate inherent in the purchase price agreed between the forfaiters for the paper itself, until the paper is repaid. If repayment is effected more quickly than the secondary forfaiter assumed, then all of the withheld sum plus the accrued interest, or that part of this total sum proportionate to the length of time by which the payment delay was less than he expected (after all, the delay may well be longer than the primary forfaiter, and therefore the higher calculation, assumed but shorter than the secondary forfaiter, and therefore the lower calculation, assumed), will be paid to the primary forfaiter. If the delay is less than even the primary forfaiter assumed, the additional sum to be paid will not, of course, be greater than the total, including interest, held in suspense, so that at least the secondary forfaiter always knows his maximum contingent liability. Similarly, if the delay is greater than even the secondary forfaiter assumed, the primary forfaiter will not be expected to make recompense: the primary forfaiter will thus have a contingent asset, the maximum amount of which he can calculate, but will not have any contingent liability.

Alternatively, the opposite approach might be agreed. In other words, the secondary forfaiter might pay over the higher sum when he buys the paper, and the primary forfaiter hold the difference between this and the lower figure in suspense, bearing interest as indicated above, until the paper is repaid. The actual delay in repayment will again determine any sum he has to pay over. He will know his maximum contingent liability and the secondary forfaiter his maximum contingent asset, since the amount to be paid will not exceed the amount held in suspense, no matter how late the paper is repaid. In this case, the primary forfaiter will have no contingent asset, however quickly repayment is actually effected.

6

Discounting methods and calculations

'Straight discount' and 'discount to yield'

The first matter to clarify when discussing discounting is the difference between the terms 'straight discount' and 'discount to yield'. A simple example best illustrates it. A straight discount of 10% applied to a bill of US$1,000,000 is US$100,000, leaving a discounted sum of US$900,000. If the bill is repayable in one year's time, this represents a yield of 100/900 or 11.11% per annum compounded annually (or a slightly lower rate if interest is compounded more frequently, say semi-annually or quarterly). A 'straight discount' of 10% can therefore be expressed as 'a discount at a rate corresponding to a yield of 11.11% compounded annually', or, more simply, as 'a discount to yield 11.11% compounded annually'.

In practice, of course, the 'discount to yield' is more useful to anyone involved in a forfaiting transaction, since the yield or interest rate is the important factor. However, because 'straight discount' is sometimes quoted, it is important to clarify which term is being used when any transaction is being discussed, and it is helpful to be able to translate one quoted figure into the other. In Appendix III, therefore, tables for the conversion of straight discounts into yields are shown.

Calculating the face value of the bills or notes to be forfaited

Once the importer and exporter have agreed that payment for the goods or services provided will be effected via a series of medium-term debt obligations, the exporter needs to establish the face value of those notes. This is simply a matter of applying the interest rate for the credit to the sale price. However, the way in which it is applied can vary. In Chapter 9, an example is shown whereby all five bills in a series except the last have equal face values, their total being £1,550,000. The cost of the goods is

£994,000 and the interest rate, compounded annually, is 16½%.

These same basic factors, cost and interest rate, could be combined in many ways to produce different payment schedules. Here are three methods commonly found.

(a)   The sale price is divided into five equal instalments of £198,800. Interest is added to each tranche on the total sum outstanding – see Table 6.1)

Table 6.1   Calculating the face value of the bills or notes to be forfaited: method (a)

Sale price	Interest at 16½% p.a. on the total outstanding	Face value of bills	Maturity at end of
£198,800	£164,010 (1)	£362,810	Year 1
198,800	131,208 (2)	330,008	Year 2
198,800	98,406	297,206	Year 3
198,800	65,604	264,404	Year 4
198,800	32,802	231,602	Year 5
£994,000	£492,030	£1,486,030	

(1) 16½% × £994,000. (2) 16½% × (994,000 − 198,800).

(b)   The sale price is divided into five equal instalments of £198,800 and interest is added to each for the whole of the period to its maturity, compounded appropriately (in this case annually) – see Table 6.2.

Table 6.2   Calculating the face value of the bills or notes to be forfaited: method (b)

Sale price	Interest at 16½% p.a. to the maturity of the bill	Face value of bills	Maturity at end of
£198,800	£32,802	£231,602 (1)	Year 1
198,800	71,016	269,816 (2)	Year 2
198,800	115,536	314,336	Year 3
198,800	167,403	366,203	Year 4
198,800	227,826	426,626	Year 5
£994,000	£614,583	£1,608,583	

(1) £198,800 × (1 + 0.165) (2) £198,800 × (1 + 0.165)^2 – i.e. two years' interest on £198,800 annually compounded using the compound interest formula FV = PV × (1 + p/100)^n where FV = future value, PV = present value, p = interest rate and n = number of periods.

(c)   Bills of equal face value are calculated using an approximate annuity formula.

Although annuity tables render an accurate annuity calculation simple to perform, this approximation is even simpler. In this example, the average life of the bills is three years: interest at $16\frac{1}{2}\%$ p.a. on £994,000 is £492,030. The five bills each have a face value, therefore, of (£994,000 + £492,030) ÷ 5 = £297,206, the total face value of the bills being £1,486,030. Of course, this method, because it is an approximation, cannot produce a precise yield of $16\frac{1}{2}\%$ and the difference can be significant.

It hardly needs stressing that the different total amounts payable by the importer, according to the method chosen, are not of themselves important. In that different methods produce different repayment profiles, any one may be more appropriate than the others to particular circumstances – for example, to the importer's expected cash flow – but each method is designed to provide the same true yield, and the different amounts payable merely reflect differences in amounts and periods outstanding over the lives of the various bills.

Calculating the discounted value of the debt obligation

Provided that the forfaiter's discount terms and the rate of interest included in the exporter's invoice price are the same, then the forfaiter in the example quoted above will discount the bills involved for £994,000. As indicated in Chapter 9, however, there is no particular reason why the two rates should be the same. Indeed, in practice, a forfaiter is often presented with bills or notes to be discounted upon which he has not previously quoted and over the interest element of which he has therefore had no influence. From the exporter's point of view, this need present no problem: if the forfaiter's discount terms include a lower interest rate than that included in the invoice price and therefore the series of bills to be forfaited, or if the sale price of the goods excluding interest provides a sufficient margin to cover a forfaiter's interest rate in excess of the interest rate the importer is prepared to pay, then the difference between the rate the exporter is paying the forfaiter and the rate he is receiving from the importer is inconsequential. Whether or not this is the case does not affect the forfaiter. He simply needs to calculate the discounted value of the series he is asked to purchase using the interest rate he is prepared to offer.

Discount formula

The price of a discounted bill is derived by discounting the face value of a bill at the interest rate (yield, *not* straight discount) specified for the appropriate term, using a discount factor which is calculated by the following formula:

$$Z = \frac{100}{100 + \left(\dfrac{d \times X}{N} \right)}$$

where Z = discount factor
N = number of days assumed in the year (for all Eurocurrency transactions this is 360)
d = interest rate
X = actual number of days in the year

Where part of a year is involved, this formula becomes

$$Z = \frac{100}{100 + \left[\dfrac{d \times (S + G)}{N} \right]}$$

where S = number of days from purchase to maturity (where a bill matures on a Sunday or Saturday or a public holiday, maturity is deemed due on the next working day)
G = number of grace days

Where the period between purchase and maturity exceeds 365 days and interest is to be compounded on an annual basis, the period needs to be broken into 365 days and the additional period and both the above formulae have to be used.

This is best illustrated by a simple example. What is the price a forfaiter will pay for the following note?

Face value	US$1,000
Maturity date	31 October 1985
Purchase date	1 August 1984
Days in year	360
Number of grace days	3
Interest rate	10.5625%
Compounding basis	Annual
Period between purchase and maturity	456 days

First, apply the appropriate formula above to the first 365 days:

$$Z_1 = \frac{100}{100 + \left(\dfrac{10.5625 \times 365}{360} \right)} = 0.90327$$

This gives a discounted value for the bill for 12 months of US$903.27 (US$1,000 × 0.90327).

Second, apply the other formula to the remaining period:

$$Z_2 = \frac{100}{100 + \left[\dfrac{10.5625 \times (91 + 3)}{360} \right]} = 0.97316$$

Finally, apply this second discount factor to the previously calculated discount value; i.e., US$903.27 × 0.97316 = US$879.02, which is the discounted value that the forfaiter will pay.

In this example, compounding has been annual. If compounding is to be, for example, semi-annual, then X needs to be split into two half-years and S similarly split to reflect any half-year periods. (1.8.84 − 1.2.85 = 184 days and 1.2.85 − 1.8.85 = 181 days.)

In this example, for the first period,

$$Z_1 = \frac{100}{100 + \left(\dfrac{10.5625 \times 184}{360} \right)} = 0.94878$$

and the first discount value is US$948.78 (US$1,000 × 0.94878).

The second semi-annual period's discount calculation is

$$Z_2 = \frac{100}{100 + \left(\dfrac{10.5625 \times 181}{360} \right)} = 0.94957$$

The discount factor for the second period, when applied to US$948.78, gives US$900.94.

The discount factor for the third period is, of course, 0.97316 ($S + G$ being less than half a year and therefore unaffected by the semi-annual compounding). Applying this to US$900.94 gives US$876.76, which is the price the forfaiter will quote.

Approximation of the discount formula

The above formula can be applied easily enough using modern electronic equipment and an appropriate program even where a series of bills is involved. However, a simpler approximation exists whereby the discount, D, is calculated by using the formula

$$D = \frac{V \times (S + G)}{100} \times \frac{d}{N}$$

where V = face value of the bill
       S = total number of days from purchase to maturity
       G = number of grace days
       d = interest rate
       N = number of days assumed in the year

In the above example,

$$D = \frac{1000 \times (456 + 3)}{100} \times \frac{10.5625}{360} = \text{US\$}134.67$$

so that the forfaiter will quote a price for the bill of US\$1,000 − US\$134.67 = US\$865.33. Although this method is inaccurate, it is frequently used by forfaiters and has the merit, from their standpoint, of tending to overstate the required discount.

Calculation of the yield implicit in a transaction

It frequently happens that a forfaiter, particularly one operating in the secondary market, is offered a bill at a given amount. Generally, his first reaction will be to ascertain the yield implicit in it. With an appropriate computer and program, this is simple. In its absence, his best course is to calculate the straight discount from the face value which the purchase price represents (see the first section of this chapter for an explanation) and use conversion tables as shown in Appendix III.

Failing this, the following formula can be used to produce an approximate figure although, the longer the period outstanding to maturity, the less accurate it is, since it works on a simple interest method rather than compound interest.

$$\text{Yield} = \frac{(R - P)}{P} \times \frac{N}{(S + G)} \times 100$$

where R = the face value of the bill
       P = the purchase price of the bill
and N, S and G are as defined above.

This formula can be adapted for a series of bills as follows. However, it is a further approximation and the caveat above as to accuracy is even more appropriate.

$$\text{Yield} = \frac{(\text{Total face value} - \text{Total purchase price}) \times 100}{\text{Total purchase price} \times \text{Weighted average remaining life of the bills}}$$

Net yield

On the face of it, establishing the net yield on a transaction is simple. For example, if paper is purchased to yield 13.50% per annum compounded annually and the forfaiter's cost of borrowing to fund the transaction is 11.75% payable annually, the net yield is 1.75%. In reality, forfaiters do not generally match paper and its funding very specifically as to maturity dates, so that a net yield calculation of this sort is the only practical possibility.

Where matching is precise, however, and loan repayments can be manipulated to utilise all cash from the maturity of all the bills in the series, the actual net yield can be seen to be somewhat higher than this. The reason is that the cash flow from the transaction is automatically being utilised: in other words, the net income is being reinvested to reduce borrowings which are therefore declining at a faster rate than the outstanding paper.

Details of a perfectly matched transaction

In the following example, the purchase of the paper took place on 27 January 1984. All grace days have been added to the maturity dates which have been adjusted for bills maturing on non-business days. The total face value of the bills is US$8,817,085.10, which is repayable over five years in ten semi-annual instalments. The bills yield 13.50% per annum compounded annually, and are funded by a loan bearing interest at 11.75% payable annually. The cash flow pertaining to this transaction is shown in Table 6.3.

Explanatory notes to Table 6.3

Column 1 shows the predetermined face values of the bills.

Column 2 shows the net values of the bills after discounting at 13.50% per annum discount to yield, compounded annually. The formula to arrive at these figures is shown above. For example, the price of the third maturity, which occurs 538 days after purchase date, is given below.

For the first whole year the discount factor,

$$Z_1 = \frac{100}{100 + \left(\dfrac{13.5 \times 365}{360} \right)} = 0.87960$$

This is multiplied by the face value of the note,
US$949,855.91 = US$835,497.23.

The discount factor for the remaining partial period of 173 days (538−365 days) is

$$Z_2 = \frac{100}{100 + \left(\dfrac{13.5 \times 173}{360} \right)} = 0.93908$$

This is multiplied by the discounted value at the end of the first whole period, US$835,497.23 = US$784,596.53.

Table 6.3   Cash flow for perfectly matched transaction

US$

Maturity	Days	Face value of bills	Discounted @ 13.5% p.a.	Loan balance	Interest @ 11.75% p.a.	Balance of principal & interest due	Repayment of principal & interest
		(1)	(2)	(3)	(4)	(5)	(6)
27.1.84	—	—	—	6,415,750.33	—	8,388,681.95	—
19.7.84	174	1,004,373.83	942,852.69	5,465,351.25	53,974.75	7,384,308.12	1,004,373.83
18.1.85	183	977,114.87	861,748.31	5,125,063.66	636,827.28	6,407,193.25	977,114.87
18.7.85	181	949,855.91	784,596.53	4,228,191.71	52,983.96	5,457,337.34	949,855.91
18.1.86	184	922,596.95	715,705.11	3,807,927.42	502,332.66	4,534,740.39	922,596.95
18.7.86	181	895,337.98	650,523.43	2,962,792.79	50,203.35	3,639,402.41	895,337.98
18.1.87	184	868,079.02	592,336.71	2,446,710.01	351,996.24	2,771,323.39	868,079.02
18.7.87	181	840,820.06	537,361.17	1,653,036.37	47,146.42	1,930,503.33	840,820.06
18.1.88	184	813,561.10	488,300.14	1,037,483.77	198,008.50	1,116,942.23	813,561.10
18.7.88	182	786,302.14	441,862.40	295,271.12	44,089.49	336,640.09	786,302.14
19.1.89	185	759,043.24	400,463.84	—	35,368.97	—	330,640.09
		8,817,085.10	6,415,750.33		1,972,931.62		8,388,681.95
		(7)	(7)		(8)		(9)

Column 3 at 27.1.84 and (7) show the sum of the discounted values of the bills which is the loan required to finance the purchase of all the bills. Column 3 at other maturities shows the balance of the loan outstanding.

Column 4 shows the interest which is charged annually on the balance of the loan outstanding, except where an instalment is paid between interest dates, in which event interest is charged from the last interest due date for the loan to the date of payment on only the principal amount repaid.

For example, the interest due on the first bill, maturing 174 days after purchase, is calculated as follows. The loan principal repayment is obtained by discounting the bill using the above formula but substituting the loan interest rate for the discount to yield rate, and by discounting for the number of days elapsed since purchase.

$$\text{Thus, the discount factor} = \frac{100}{100 + \left(\dfrac{11.75 \times 174}{360} \right)} = 0.94626$$

This is multiplied by the face value of the bill,
US\$1,004,373.83 = US\$950,399.08.

The interest payment is the face value less repayment of loan principal

$$
\begin{array}{r}
\text{US\$1,004,373.83} \\
\text{US\$\ \ 950,399.08} \\
\hline
\text{US\$\ \ \ \ 53,974.75}
\end{array}
$$

In this example, the first interest period ends on 18 January 1985, at the second maturity, and occurs $174 + 183 \ (= 357)$ days after purchase. Interest is calculated as follows.

$$\text{Interest} = \frac{\begin{array}{c}\text{Number of days since}\\\text{last interest date}\end{array}}{360} \times \begin{array}{c}\text{Loan balance}\\\text{outstanding}\end{array} \times \begin{array}{c}\text{Interest rate}\\\text{per annum}\end{array}$$

Substituting the figures from the example,

$$\text{Interest} = \frac{357}{360} \times 5,465,351.25 \times \frac{11.75}{100} = \text{US\$636,827.28}$$

The loan principal repayable at an interest payment date is the face value of the bill less the interest calculated above.

The interest calculations are applied to alternate maturities to obtain the total interest due, denoted by (8).

Column 5 at 27.1.84 and (9) show the total amount needed to pay the total principal and total interest due (denoted by (7) and (8) respectively). Column 5 at other maturities shows the interest and principal outstanding after deducting the proceeds of any matured bills (denoted by column 1), and is required for calculation purposes.

Column 6 shows that the amount of the maturing face value of each bill is applied in reduction of interest and then principal.

From the above, only the last bill generates the actual 'cash' profit – the entire proceeds of all other bills are applied in repayment of the loan.

The advantage of this method of funding is that the loan is paid off as rapidly as possible and the cash profit is fixed with no exposure to changes in interest rates.

Additionally, there is no negative cash flow at any stage throughout the life of the transaction.

The question arises as to the true yield implicit in this perfectly matched transaction. There are two methods by which it may be calculated.

(a) The interest profit is obtained by deducting the total of the discounted value of all bills from the total face value of all bills.

In this example, this is	US$ 8,817,085.10
minus	US$ 6,415,750.33
	US$ 2,401,334.77
Next, deduct the total interest expense	US$ 1,972,931.62
Interest profit	US$ 428,403.15

Next, calculate the weighted average life of the series of bills. In this example, this is 948.8 days or 2.6356 years (based on a 360-day year).

To obtain the yield, divide the interest profit by the discounted value of the bills and divide the result by the average life.

$$\text{Yield} = \frac{428,403.15}{6,415,750.33} \times \frac{100}{2.6356}$$

$$= 2.5335\% \text{ per annum}$$

(b) The net-cash-flow column in Table 6.4 is obtained as follows.

For period 0, this amount is the 'pay away' or investment figure and is represented by the total of the discounted value of all notes in the series. It is also equal to the loan.

For periods 1 to 10, these amounts are the maturing face value of each note less the funding interest applicable to each period and represent the repayment and the return on the 'investment'.

Table 6.4   *Obtaining an accurate estimate of the yield*

Number of days outstanding	Semi-annual period	Net cash flow
	0	−6,415,750.33
174	1	950,399.08
357	2	340,287.59
538	3	896,871.95
722	4	420,264,29
903	5	845,134.63
1,087	6	516,082.78
1,268	7	793,673.64
1,452	8	615,552.60
1,634	9	742,212.65
1,819	10	723,674.27
		428,403.15

Solving for the internal rate of return gives the following results.

Rate per period: 1.1909%
Nominal rate per annum: 2.3819%
Effective rate per annum: 2.3960%

The difference in the yield obtained via this method from that derived in (a) arises from the fact that the above method recognises the actual cash flow of the transaction and does not estimate the yield based upon total net income over average life. This second method should be used if an accurate assessment of the yield is required.

The point of most significance is, as intimated earlier, that the true net yield on such a transaction is approximately 2.4% per annum, rather than 1.75%, as might be assumed from paper yielding 13.50% funded by a loan at 11.75%. However, it must be stressed that most à forfait transactions do not lend themselves to a net yield calculation of this sort because the purchase and its funding are seldom so matched that cash flow can be projected in this manner.

7

Managing à forfait transactions – risks to exporters, importers and guarantors

Now that the principles and practical application of à forfait finance have been described, it is appropriate to consider in more detail the management and accounting control risks which anyone involved in a forfaiting deal as exporter, importer or guarantor runs as well as suggesting methods of minimising them. It must be understood that reference to risks in this chapter does not involve legal difficulties or pitfalls peculiar to à forfait financing, since these are dealt with in Chapter 4 and examples involving such problems are given in Chapter 10. In Chapter 8, risks run by forfaiters are dealt with and, again, methods of management and accounting controls which forfaiters can and should implement in order to avoid or circumscribe these risks are set out.

The exporter's risks

An exporter who has sold an amount receivable to a forfaiter has virtually no outstanding risk arising from the transaction. His only risks may arise during the period between the acceptance of his tender or bid for the importer's custom and the delivery of the goods or services, that is, during a period when he is committed to taking à forfait finance at an agreed discount rate even though the contract with the importer has yet to be completed. Any interest-rate risk during this period should not, however, be overemphasised as it only represents an 'opportunity' risk. In other words, if the exporter did not commit himself to the finance, he would be able to obtain a more favourable discount rate in the event that interest rates declined: but, since his tender will have been submitted after taking account of the finance costs he has accepted, the opportunity cost is effectively offset by the opportunity profits on the marginally higher contract price he has negotiated than that which he would have sought with the benefit of those lower rates.

There is the risk, of course, that the importer will arbitrarily cancel the contract during the commitment period or that, for some other reason, the contract will not be completed. In this event, the exporter is obliged to recompense the forfaiter for any cost or loss he suffers. In practice, a forfaiter will generally look upon the problem sympathetically, if only because he wants to maintain his relationship with the exporter. In addition, it is probably fair to say that any question of compensation for the forfaiter is usually trivial compared with the problems which caused the cancellation in the first place and with any sum which the aggrieved party, importer or exporter, is seeking from the other as a consequence. Finally, there is no control which can be instituted by the exporter to protect himself against this risk.

The one true risk that the exporter may run during the commitment period arises when the promissory notes or bills of exchange which he has agreed to sell are denominated in a currency other than his own reporting currency. He will have the risk that currency movements will be unfavourable to him. In fact, of course, this is not a risk specific to à forfait finance, since most contracts in a foreign currency, however they are to be financed, involve it. It can always be avoided by a specific provision in the tender document which allows for price variation in line with currency movements until the acceptance of the goods. In this case, there will almost inevitably be a slight delay in the forfaiting process, since the amounts involved will need to be calculated according to the currency parity rates at the date of acceptance.

Controlling the exporter's risks

The exporter should maintain a list of his forfaiting commitments by currency so that he can monitor his exposure to currency parity movements and enter into forward currency contracts if appropriate. As in the case of the importer and explained below, an exporter with large numbers of commitments expiring at different dates may need to list them by maturity tranche net of any forward currency contracts.

The importer's risks

Once he is committed to pay a promissory note or bill of exchange, the importer is bound, as an obligor, to make payment at a specific time in the future. The amount involved and the currency in which it is denoted are fixed. He has no risk from fluctuating interest rates, since interest on his debt is already calculated and included in the value of the bill or note itself. Provided that the currency of the bill or note is the same as that in which his accounts are reported, usually his home currency, he has no risk from currency parity movements. He will, however, be exposed to currency risk if, for example, because his home currency is obscure and no forfaiter is prepared to advance medium-term funds in it, the bill or note is denominated in some other currency. In this case, he must consider taking out forward currency contracts to hedge his exposed currency debt position, but an appropriate forward market is unlikely to be available if his home currency is obscure. He may, therefore, have a risk which can be monitored but not eliminated.

The only other risk to the importer is the possibility that he will have insufficient funds available to effect repayment on the due dates. This risk can be minimised by careful monitoring of his cash and debt positions.

Controlling the importer's risks

Currency risk

The importer should maintain an up-to-date list in each currency of outstanding debt commitments and obligations. Any hedging foreign currency transactions should be offset against the currency totals so that the true currency exposure is shown.

Where the importer has many medium-term debt commitments and obligations maturing at various dates, and, perhaps, several forward currency contracts hedging certain of these obligations, the list may need to be split into maturity tranches – for example, debts and hedging contracts maturing within two weeks, those maturing within two weeks beyond that, and those maturing in the following month, three months or six months – so that net exposure by maturity period can be easily evaluated.

Repayment or liquidity risk

This is, in essence, the same as any other cash-flow risk that an importer or, indeed, any trader has. All businesses need to manage and monitor their cash flow. The only slight additional problem in the case of à forfait finance is that debts are due in the future rather than immediately, so that there is a greater possibility that they will be overlooked. The use of maturity lists by currency, as mentioned under 'Currency risk' above, when calculating the treasurer's cash-flow projections will reduce this possibility.

The guarantor's risks

In any à forfait transaction, the guarantor has a commitment to pay off the promissory notes or bills of exchange at their maturity dates and the right to demand simultaneous payment by the importer. It follows that he has a contingent liability and a contingent asset. Provided that both are disposed of simultaneously, he has no risk. To the extent that the importer pays late, he will demand interest for late payment and will thus be unlikely to have a significant exposure to interest charges. However, he has an absolute risk of default by the importer and an absolute sovereign risk if the importer's country is different from his own (though it is unusual for this to be the case). In the event of either late payment or non-payment, he has a liquidity risk in that he must be sure that he has adequate funds available to pay the bills or notes.

Controlling the guarantor's risks

Risk of default by the importer

The most effective control is the establishment of credit limits for individual customers and for total exposure to any industry. Any request for a guarantee by an importer can then be evaluated in the context of these limits. Credit analysis leading to the limits to be set is not the subject of this book. Suffice to say that any guarantor must have clear procedures set out in writing which must be followed, that levels of personnel who can approve limits of a praticular size must also be specified, and that any breach of limits must be reported at an appropriate level very quickly.

Sovereign risk

Similar considerations are relevant here, the only point to be mentioned being the obvious one that sovereign limits will be much larger and often subject to more frequent reconsideration than those for individual customers or particular industries.

Liquidity risk

Since most guarantors are major banks, this is seldom a matter for great concern. None the less, any guarantor will wish to maintain an up-to-date list of his contingent assets and liabilities with immediate exception reporting of any repayments that are overdue. Responsibility for reviewing exception reports and taking appropriate action must be clearly established at an appropriate level of authority.

Obviously, any exception reporting is only as good as those who monitor it. This truism is applicable to all the control mechanisms suggested in this chapter and, indeed, to those outlined in Chapter 8. Senior management must accept and act upon its responsibility to ensure that the controls instituted are being used properly. In forfaiting, as in all business, failure to do so could be expensive.

8

Managing à forfait transactions – risks to forfaiters

The forfaiter's risks

From the moment he grants an option for à forfait finance to the moment the forfaited assets are repaid, the forfaiter is exposed to risk. The various stages giving rise to risk can be charted as follows.

Option period

During the option period, the forfaiter runs the risk that interest rates will move against him. Since the exporter is not committed to the transaction at this point, the forfaiter will hardly ever enter into any funding arrangements in respect of it. His exposure is thus absolute.

By the same token, the forfaiter has accepted the credit-worthiness of the guarantor as soon as he grants the option. He is exposed to risk in this respect and to sovereign risk until he is repaid or until the exporter refuses the option.

Commitment period

The only thing that changes, in terms of risk, between the option period and the commitment period is that the forfaiter can assume in the commitment period that the à forfait transaction will take place. He can therefore commit himself to funding arrangements and, assuming he can obtain fixed-rate funding, thereby eliminate any interest-rate risk. In practice, most forfaiters do not do this, waiting instead until they buy the forfaited assets before funding the purchase. Indeed, most forfaiters seem not at any stage to match their funding completely to the maturities of the forfaited assets in their portfolio, tending to prefer to 'borrow short and lend long'. In this, they mirror the approach adopted by major banks in the United Kingdom and in some other countries.

The rationale seems to be that, in the absence of likely adverse movements in the cost of their funding, it is sensible to do this because short interest rates are generally lower than those for the longer term. In addition, in some currencies in which they deal, forfaiters would probably have difficulty obtaining five to seven-year funding at any price and there might well be difficulty in borrowing at a fixed rate for such periods in any currency.

But perhaps the most significant reason for not matching funding too closely to the maturities of forfaited assets is the flexibility it enables the forfaiter to retain. If he sees an attractive opportunity to sell some of his assets on the secondary market, the forfaiter does not wish to be drawn into difficult and potentially expensive negotiations to free himself of any related funding.

Last, forfaiters will claim the right to make judgements about interest trends and maintain that, should those trends appear adverse, they can then make the appropriate funding decisions: in other words, not matching maturities with fixed-rate borrowings upon the inception of an à forfait deal or upon commitment does not preclude the forfaiter from doing so if it seems appropriate later on. This approach will certainly afford the forfaiter the opportunity to take advantage of any declines in interest rates during the life of the forfaited assets he is holding, or even during the commitment period.

In reality, then, the interest-rate risk noted above as existing during the option period is seldom mitigated during the commitment period or when the asset is actually bought.

Date of purchase

Until this date is reached, the forfaiter can always back out of the à forfait transaction if he finds irregularities in the asset he is buying or in its guarantee or, indeed, if he is dissatisfied as to the completion of formalities in respect of the particular transaction, for example failure by the importer to obtain the permission of the relevant authorities for the commitment to transfer the relevant foreign currency at the maturity dates of the bills or notes forfaited. Once he has paid for the assets, even though he may have legal redress against some other party to the transaction, he is exposed to the risk that the asset he has bought will prove defective. Apart from doing what he can to ensure that all the documentation surrounding the transaction is adequate, therefore, he will be anxious to limit the exposure he has to the trustworthiness and competence of the importer and the exporter and, as shown by the first case history in Chapter 10, in extreme cases to their credit-worthiness as well.

Another risk may arise from the method which the forfaiter uses to fund the purchase. In most cases, he will borrow in the same currency as that of the paper to be bought, but this is not necessarily the case. If he borrows, for example, Deutschmarks, swaps these via a foreign currency contract for US dollars and uses these to buy US dollar paper, then he automatically exposes himself to a foreign exchange risk by having a US dollar asset and a Deutschmark liability. Provided that his funding and the paper have simultaneous maturities, he can hedge this exposure simply enough by entering into a forward foreign exchange contract which enables him to swap the US dollars he will receive upon the repayment of the paper into Deutschmarks to repay his borrowing.

As noted above, however, a forfaiter tends not to match his borrowings and his assets sufficiently closely for this to be a realistic possibility, so that any forward hedging contract he does take out represents merely an impure swap. That is, it either swaps US dollars expected from the repayment of maturing paper into Deutschmarks which cannot be specifically earmarked against maturing borrowings or buys Deutschmarks to repay borrowings, although the US dollars to be sold cannot be specifically related to any maturing assets.

In this case, the forfaiter has not hedged his total exposure to currency parity movements even though his overall currency position in Deutschmarks and US dollars is square, but he has reduced it: to the extent that forward interest rates in US dollars and Deutschmarks vary between future periods – in other words, long-term and short-term interest rates do not move by the same amount – and to the extent that these variations are reflected in currency parities, the 'maturity gap' between the assets and liabilities partially hedged in this way will produce a gain or a loss. On any individual transaction, such a gain or loss is unlikely to be large, but the amount involved in the case of a substantial portfolio may be significant and certainly needs to be watched.

Of course, a forfaiter will, in many instances, forgo any attempt at even a partial hedge of this nature. He may well be content to run foreign currency positions arising from a particular à forfait transaction, unmatched either in total or within maturity periods, provided that the overall total foreign currency position he has is small. Again, the important point is that he be aware of the positions he is running so that he limits his exposure to that acceptable to him.

Period during which paper is held

Apart from the risks noted above, the one very obvious danger that the forfaiter faces while he has the asset is that he will fail to send maturing assets for collection. An oversight in this respect is seldom tragic, but any delay in receiving repayment costs the forfaiter money.

The other side of the coin is that the forfaiter needs to keep a careful watch on his borrowings to ensure that he has funds available to pay them when they become due, since, as stated earlier, he is unlikely to have matched the repayment of his borrowings to the maturity dates of his assets.

Date of maturity of the paper

The only additional risk at this point in the life of an à forfait transaction arises from its late payment because of tardiness or incompetence on the part of the guarantor or his paying agent. It is true that, if this happens, the forfaiter has grounds to make a claim for interest on the offending party, but it is also true that he may have great difficulty in actually obtaining the interest.

Controlling the forfaiter's risks

Interest-rate risk

The forfaiter needs to maintain an up-to-date list by currency of all items in his portfolio and those for which he has extended an option or to which he is committed. This list can be subdivided into maturity tranches. Against the total of each tranche can be set borrowings which are to be repaid in that period, net of new borrowings committed for draw-down. Average borrowing rates and average earning rates by tranche can be calculated, so that the net margin is apparent. By his knowledge of prevailing interest rates, any reviewer of this list will see immediately whether or not new borrowing needed at any point in the future is likely to be at a higher or lower rate than that being earned by the assets, and at a higher or lower rate than his existing borrowing. It will help him reach an informed judgement as to his best course of action in maximising the net return on his portfolio.

Because of his general tendency not to match borrowings specifically to the maturity of assets, a forfaiter may well have some assets, purchased at a time of relatively low interest rates, which are earning less than the prevailing cost of borrowing as a result of an increase in interest rates. Since a forfaiter in this position will probably be looking upon his portfolio as a pool of assets, this will not disturb him greatly, provided that, overall, his portfolio is profitable. However, highlighting such assets by the use of this interest-rate risk report is valuable, not as a cautionary parable, but to provide impetus in determining an appropriate method of remedying the situation – for example, by seeking their early sale. It is obvious that the list must be comprehensive in both the borrowings and the assets it shows. Each time it is produced, therefore, their totals should be agreed to the amounts shown in the currency balance sheets with appropriate adjustment for options and commitments.

Appendix IV contains an example of an interest-rate risk report.

Of course, this represents a method merely of controlling rather than eliminating interest-rate risk. A forfaiter, as already stated, may have rejected or may simply not have had the opportunity to obtain fixed-rate funding which would have removed the risk entirely. If fixed-rate finance is not available to him, even though he would take it if given the chance, he should consider the possibility of accepting variable-rate funding to match the maturities of the forfaited assets he is purchasing and hedging it with interest-rate futures.

The mechanism by which this would operate to provide him with something akin to fixed-rate borrowing is explained in Chapter 2 in the context of possible alternative sources of fixed-rate finance for exporters and thus will not be repeated here. Its limitations do bear repetition, however. The futures instruments available are severely limited in both their maturity periods and the currencies in which they are denominated; medium-term futures instruments and variable-rate borrowing will have somewhat divergent interest trends.

In practice, therefore, this is seldom accepted by forfaiters at present as a variable method of fixing interest rates on their borrowings. As the available futures instruments increase in range and as they become more widely traded throughout the financial markets of the world, however, they are likely to become more valuable to forfaiters. For this reason, the forfaiter is well advised to bear them in mind when seeking fixed-rate finance.

Guarantor credit risk

Just as the guarantor should have set credit limits for individual customers and industries (see Chapter 7), so the forfaiter should set credit limits for individual guarantors. The forfaiter should have clear procedures set out in writing for establishing these limits, levels of personnel who can approve limits of a particular size must be specified, and any breach of those limits must be reported at an appropriate level very quickly. One important point to remember is that limits ascribed to guarantors should not always be decided in isolation: a forfaiter may be part of an organisation, for example a bank, which has many dealings in different contexts with a guarantor, who is very likely also to be a bank. Any credit limit must therefore take account of the whole organisation's total exposure to the guarantor. Failure to do this may have the unfortunate result that the forfaiting organisation's exposure is several times that originally intended. There should therefore be a centrally produced credit limit report which shows all the credit and guarantee facilities available to each customer and the amounts drawn down under each category.

Sovereign risk

Documentation which establishes sovereign risk limits and outlines levels of authority to approve them, the importance of ensuring compliance with them and the necessity to ensure all forms of credit are taken into account in using those limits, are, broadly, as outlined above. However, where sovereign risk is concerned, there is an even more fundamental point to make than these. Which country represents the risk? In most circumstances, the answer will simply be that of the guarantor and this will generally be the same as that of the importer.

Which country is that of the guarantor? The difficulty sometimes encountered in answering this apparently simple question can be illustrated by considering the case of a guarantor which is an overseas branch of a British bank. There seems little doubt that, legally, any obligation of a branch is an obligation of its head office. However, in the event that the cash to effect repayment of forfaited assets cannot be transferred from that overseas country, it may not always be possible to invoke a claim against the head office. For example, if the guaranteeing branch transferred the funds to the central bank of that country for transmission to the forfaiter, and the central bank withheld payment because of foreign exchange shortages or a general debt crisis, then the forfaiter would probably not succeed in forcing payment by the head office. Any attempt to do so through the courts would probably lead to the response that the action had to be decided in favour of the head office, because the payment by the guarantor to his central bank extinguished the debt under the guarantor's local law and therefore the forfaiter had no claim remaining against the branch. Any claim lay simply against the central bank and, clearly, such a claim could not be pursued against the head office.

To take another example, it is quite usual for the head office of a bank to accept the obligation of a foreign subsidiary as its own, largely to maintain good relations with its customers and their correspondent banks. However, the legal position of a subsidiary is different from that of a branch in that the guarantee of the former is not that of its head office. In this instance, the head office's general policy not to take advantage of the legal position means that the sovereign risk is arguably that of the country in which the head office is situated.

In both these instances, the real sovereign risk is the opposite of that which the law would imply. Careful consideration must always be given to the question of where the risk lies: experience of the guarantor is, of course, a help, but it is not always an adequate guide to his or his head office's future action.

As a further thought in relation to the vexed question of sovereign risk, it is important to remember that this is one of the components which determines the interest rate a forfaiter will seek on a forfaiting proposal, as stated in Chapter 5. Ambiguity or doubt in this respect, therefore, may have a direct effect on the forfaiter's income quite apart from any losses from default. From all points of view, therefore, it is important to assess sovereign risk correctly.

However careful the assesment of sovereign risk, however good the procedures for monitoring it and however conscientious those responsible for reviewing it may be, none of this can in itself remove the risk entirely. In some countries, insurance policies against sovereign risk may be available at certain times. Naturally, such policies tend only to be available in respect of less risky countries – although insurers would presumably claim that anything can be insured at a price – and are thus of limited value. Many forfaiters would claim, too, that they have never used insurance against sovereign risk because the detailed provisions of those policies that they could use are too restricted or the premiums are too high. However, this is a potential method the forfaiter could use to eliminate his sovereign risk and therefore he must always consider it.

Risk of inadequate documentation

This risk can best be controlled by the use of a check-list covering such matters as evidence to support the genuineness and legality of the trade underlying the forfaiting transaction, checks which need to be made on the form and content stipulated by the guarantor's local law of any letter of guarantee or aval, and checks ascertaining local requirements which are needed to gain permission for the remittance of foreign currency.

A procedure should be stipulated in writing for the completion and review of such a check-list and also for methodical and timely follow-up of any inadequacies in documentation which this process throws up. While there can be no substitute for a forfaiter's experience and knowledge in these matters, evidence that he has satisfactory internal procedures which have been followed in dealing with matters of this sort has the aditional merit of helping to disprove any allegations of negligence which a primary forfaiter selling into the secondary market may face if an à forfait transaction goes wrong.

Exporter and importer risks

It was stated in Chapter 3 that a forfaiter will generally examine the competence, credibility and credit-worthiness of these parties to a forfaiting transaction only very superficially, since he will very seldom have need to revert to them because of a problem. To the extent that the exporter or importer is known to him from previous dealings, or from general reputation, any specific steps that he need take to check them out will be further reduced. The important thing is that he must make a conscious decision as to what constitutes an appropriate procedure for checking them, bearing in mind that the overriding objective is to develop a comprehensive understanding of the business transacted and a close knowledge of the companies involved.

This procedure should be specified in writing and, again, a check-list is a useful tool for ensuring that it has been followed. He may wish to talk to their bankers and/or review their latest published or management accounts. He is very likely to want to visit the exporter's premises and talk to senior personnel. Although he will usually need to expend little time or effort carrying out such work, failure to do it exposes him to unnecessary risk, since there always remains the possibility, however remote, that he will need to seek financial redress from either or both of these parties. In addition, as mentioned in the previous section, a properly completed and comprehensive check-list is proof for the primary forfaiter against any allegations of negligence from those in the secondary market.

Currency risk

The forfaiter needs to maintain an up-to-date list by currency of all his forward currency contracts by maturity period. The total by tranche can be offset against assets, liabilities, options and commitments maturing in those periods, thereby enabling the forfaiter to assess immediately his 'gap positions'. (This information appears in the liquidity report which is circulated to the à forfait dealers referred to below. An example of a liquidity report appears in Appendix IV.) The total in each currency of his forward positions, options and commitments should be included in an overall position sheet along with net assets and liabilities in those currencies, to arrive at a net total position by currency. These two records, gap position and total position, enable the forfaiter to determine his exposure to currency movements and to take any necessary remedial action. Needless to say, it is important that someone with the appropriate understanding has the specific responsibility to monitor them.

It is interesting to note that a forfaiter might well believe that his total net position in any one foreign currency is small, whereas this is not really the case. He may have forgotten to include incoming profits on forfaiting transactions and outgoing interest payments. Indeed, it is often true of banks that they omit cover for their foreign currency earnings, suddenly discovering a substantial uncovered position. This emphasises the importance of the total position record and of ensuring that the net assets and liabilities shown on it agree with the forfaiter's balance sheet in each currency.

Naturally, accuracy is vital in the lists of outstanding foreign currency contracts, too. Therefore, periodically, if not each time the lists are produced, their total should be agreed with the foreign exchange department's records or, if this is the source of their preparation, with accounting records.

There is an example of a total currency position report in Appendix IV.

Collection risk

The first method of limiting this risk is the 'grace period' explained in Chapter 5.

Apart from this, the forfaiter must have a person specifically responsible for tracking maturity dates and sending bills and notes for collection at the appropriate time. It is preferable that the source of his information be the company's accounting records so that he can be sure that no items are omitted from his list, but, whatever the source, he must tie total outstandings into the accounts frequently, preferably daily.

Liquidity risk

The interest-rate risk report and the foreign currency contracts list together provide the forfaiter with most of the cash-flow information he requires to minimise the risk of lack of liquidity. Most forfaiters designate a particular individual as treasurer with the responsibility both for monitoring this information and for taking the action necessary to overcome any looming cash difficulties. It is, of course, most important that he and those conducting the actual forfaiting business are in constant contact, in order that the company is not committed to new à forfait deals which it cannot fulfil. For this reason, it is most satisfactory for the liquidity report the treasurer maintains to be circulated to the à forfait dealers each day with a note of remaining available borrowing facilities. The accuracy of this report must, of course, be checked periodically by balancing its components against accounting and/or the dealers' records.

An example of a liquidity report is shown in Appendix IV.

Other risks

This chapter would be incomplete without some mention of one or two more obvious risks which are not unique to forfaiting but which are often either overlooked or inadequately controlled.

Safe keeping of assets

It is unlikely that promissory notes or bills of exchange held by a forfaiter will be subject to theft. Not only would the thief need to obtain the documents, but he would also have to arrange either that payment for them at maturity be directed to him or that another party, probably a forfaiter, buys them without suspicion. An individual would be most unlikely to achieve either, not least because the amount involved in any single tranche of forfaited paper is normally substantial, and an attempt to sell or obtain funds would almost inevitably raise large question marks.

Pieces of paper can be lost or burnt, however. The first safeguard, therefore, is a strong fire-proof safe in which to keep them and the number of company personnel with access to the safe should be limited. Second, there should be a log of all movements to and from the safe. Third, frequently but irregularly, the contents of the safe should be reconciled to the details shown by the log and agreed to the company's books of account: ideally, these steps should be performed by someone who does not normally have access to the safe or who is responsible for maintaining accounting records. It is important to remember that a primary forfaiter may well be holding forfaited paper on behalf of secondary forfaiters: this paper must be similarly controlled and accounted for. Fourth, the forfaiter must maintain adequate fire, loss and theft insurance and must review his policies regularly to ensure that they are sufficient to cover increases in his turnover and in the size of individual transactions: note that the cost of such insurance will not be high, as its purpose will be to cover interest and 'inconvenience' losses rather than the loss of the face value of the paper itself.

Unauthorised trading

In any financial trading organisation, there is the possibility of unauthorised trading by personnel either for personal enrichment or to cover their own trading errors. For the reason stated above, it is unlikely that an individual will have an opportunity to make money dishonestly from forfaited paper.

Diversion of commitment or option fees, however, may be possible, and suppression of bad deals, either in forfaited paper or in foreign exchange, too: and it is always worth remembering the numerous famous instances of dishonest foreign exchange dealing in quite recent times.

There are certain basic methods by which a forfaiter can limit his exposure in this regard.

1. He must ensure an adequate segregation of responsibilities between staff: the accounting, dealing and cash-transfer functions should be in different hands and the handling of documents and collection procedures should represent a fourth separate function.

2. There should be dual control over telex facilities, the pass-key notation being changed at frequent but irregular intervals.

3. Incoming mail and incoming and outgoing telex messages, particularly those transmitted overnight, should be reviewed periodically by top management and without prior warning.

4. Dealing slips, both for à forfait transactions themselves and for foreign exchange and borrowings, should be pre-numbered and all numbers used should occasionally be accounted for by someone independent of the dealing room.

5. Bank signatories should be limited in number, dual signatures of senior non-dealing personnel being required for all à forfait, borrowing and foreign exchange transactions.

6. Senior dealing and accounting personnel should have regular meetings with top management to establish a clear understanding of objectives and to examine reported profits in the context of budgets, expectations and known deals: it is surprising how often errors or bad deals are illuminated by such discussions.

7. Though this is probably a good theory which is very difficult to implement in practice, top management should have a sufficiently close knowledge of their subordinates' lifestyles to determine whether or not they seem curiously lavish in the light of their known incomes.

8. Key personnel should be fidelity bonded and the forfaiter must keep all insurance against malpractice by his staff under review to ensure its adequacy, given the level of activity of the company and the size of its deals.

It must be recognised that forfaiting companies often have few personnel, so that the above suggestions may be difficult or impossible to follow. In a sense, this is a safeguard in itself, since the top management of any small company will inevitably have a close relationship with other personnel and will generally be involved in decisions on matters big and small. Controlling risk in such an environment is usually easier than in a large concern.

9

Accounting and tax
in à forfait finance

This chapter deals principally with the appropriate methods of accounting for à forfait transactions by exporters, importers, forfaiters and guarantors. However, quite apart from the accounting records which each of these participants needs to maintain, they need to keep some record of their commitments to forfaiting deals. In addition, all participants should maintain a record of paper the settlement of which is outstanding. These various sundry records are dealt with briefly later on in this chapter. Finally, it outlines general taxation principles applicable to à forfait transactions.

Accounting by the exporter

An exporter entering an à forfait transaction may have two separate sorts of financial item to account for in consequence – option and/or commitment fees and the debt obligation itself.

Fees

As explained in Chapter 5, option and commitment fees are generally both payable, at least in part in the case of commitment fees, as soon as the option or commitment is granted by the forfaiter. Both are usually set at a percentage of the amount to be discounted. However, an option fee is normally a flat percentage, that is, it is unrelated to time, while a commitment fee is normally annualised. On this basis, therefore, it would appear that an option fee need not be spread over the period to which it relates, whereas a commitment fee should be: an option fee is fixed simply by the granting of an option, but a commitment fee is fixed by the length of the commitment period.

It is questionable whether an accountant would be as categorical as this implies in determining the consequent accounting treatment, but it is probably appropriate to suggest that an option fee be debited in total to the exporter's relevant expense account as soon as the option is granted. If the fee is not payable immediately, it should nevertheless be accrued in total at that point. A commitment fee, on the other hand, should be debited to a balance sheet suspense account and amortised to the exporter's relevant expense account over the commitment period in amounts proportionate to the outstanding commitment (since the total commitment may be drawn down in instalments by the exporter). Again, any commitment fee not immediately payable but chargeable immediately should be accrued.

In practice, an exporter may conclude that option and commitment fees payable are small enough to be immaterial to his accounts and that he can simply charge them both directly to his expense accounts when they are billed or, even, when they are paid. In so far as this does not accord with good accounting, he should be aware that his auditors are likely to disapprove.

The final point to be made is that both sorts of fees are simply costs of obtaining finance and should thus be debited to a financial expenses caption in the exporter's accounts.

The debt obligation or amount receivable for the goods or services provided

When he has delivered his goods or services, an exporter renders a bill. In the case of a transaction which is to be forfaited, this bill will generally be paid either via promissory notes or bills of exchange maturing in the future. The bill will, therefore, include an element of interest for the period (usually periods) of credit the exporter is extending. Assuming that the exporter has arranged the forfaiting before agreeing terms with the importer, this interest will probably have been set at the amount by which the bills or notes will be discounted by the forfaiter. In other words, the interest income incorporated in the face value of the debt obligations will equal the interest expense the exporter bears in the forfaiting process.

This need not be so, however. For example, the sale price of the goods or services provided might have been increased for credit by an amount greater than the discount the forfaiter requires. The additional figure, received by the exporter as soon as the forfaiter buys the bills or notes, represents net interest income. As windfall financing income, it should be allocated to an appropriate finance caption in the exporter's accounts. Alternatively, there might be a net cost which, similarly, should be debited to an appropriate finance caption. Whether or not this actually happens will usually depend upon the accounting treatment the exporter originally accorded to his sale transaction. If he segregated the sale price and interest income elements of the transaction correctly, then it is likely that the entire accounting treatment will be as suggested here. If he did not, but merely treated the whole sale invoice figure as sale price, then it is likely that the net interest income or cost will be misallocated.

An example will explain the point. Assume goods worth £1 million are sold on extended credit, interest charged being £200,000. Assume further that the sale invoice, payable via promissory notes, total face amount £1,200,000, is sold for £1,030,000 to a forfaiter. It is apparent that the net interest income to the exporter is £30,000 and that this figure should be credited to interest income in his accounts. If the exporter made the entries

Dr. Debtors	£1,200,000
Cr. Sales	1,000,000
Cr. Interest suspense	200,000

upon raising the invoice and the entries

Dr. Cash	£1,030,000
Dr. Interest suspense	170,000
Cr. Debtors	1,200,000

upon receiving proceeds from the forfaiter, then the net sum to be transferred from interest suspense to interest income – £30,000 credit – is correct. If, however, his original entries were Dr. Debtors £1,200,000, Cr. Sales £1,200,000 then the transfer from interest suspense – £170,000 debit – is wrong and, of course, sales are overstated by £200,000.

It should also be noted that, even in instances where the interest income and expense are equal, for example where forfaiting arrangements are settled at the outset and the relevant interest costs built into the invoice, such a misallocation could still occur. In fact, in such a case it may be less likely, simply because an exporter, knowing that his sale invoice will be subjected to a forfaiting transaction at a set amount, may short-cut his accounting entries as follows. (The above example has to be modified, of course, since the sale figure and the sum received from the forfaiter must be the same, assumed here to be £1,000,000.)

Dr. Debtors	£1,000,000	
Cr. Sales	1,000,000	at the date of delivery.
Dr. Cash	1,000,000	
Cr. Debtors	1,000,000	at the date upon which the forfaiter pays.

This point should not be dismissed as insignificant. Where extended-term credit is involved, interest figures are usually substantial. A misalloca-tion of the sort outlined above can, therefore, be significant to the exporter's accounts. A series of such errors might well be highly material but, even if not, can have serious effects upon reported profit margins and financing costs.

Accounting by the importer

An importer involved in an à forfait transaction will similarly have two separate financial items to account for, the guarantee fee and the debt obligation.

The guarantee fee

As noted in Chapter 5, a guarantee fee is normally charged at an annualised percentage of the outstanding guarantee, that is, the face value of the unmatured bills or notes. The important point is that the fee is payable in respect of the time for which the guarantee is extant. The appropriate accounting treatment for the importer, therefore, is to debit the fee to a balance sheet suspense account and amortise it to the relevant expense account over the guarantee period in amounts proportionate to the face value of the bills or notes outstanding. Any guarantee fee due but not charged should be accrued. In practice, an importer may conclude that guarantee fees chargeable are small enough to be immaterial to his accounts and that he can therefore charge them directly to expense when they are billed or, even, when they are paid. As stated in respect of option and commitment fees borne by the exporter, this may not be good accounting practice and auditors may disapprove.

Finally, guarantee fees are a cost of obtaining finance and should be debited to a financial expenses caption in the importer's accounts.

The debt obligation or amount payable to the forfaiter

As already explained in this book, the amount payable to the forfaiter upon the maturity of forfaited debt obligations will generally be routed via the guarantor. In other words, the guarantor will pay the forfaiter and the importer will repay the guarantor. This does not, of course, affect the accounting treatment in the importer's books.

The amount the importer has to pay is simply the face value of the forfaited debt instruments. However, this incorporates interest for the period of credit. This interest element must, of course, be spread over the period for which the credit is provided. The forfaiter and exporter may both know the interest rate and the amount of interest involved, but the forfaiter may not, since, as indicated in the previous section, the exporter may have calculated the interest he is charging before discussing any forfaiting arrangements: in any event, there is no particular reason that the interest rate incorporated in the exporter's invoice should be the same as that applied to the à forfait transaction by the forfaiter. Whatever knowledge the forfaiter has of the interest rate incorporated in the face value of the bills or notes he is buying, it is quite possible that the importer will not know it, however.

The first question, therefore, may be the rate of interest the importer should assume. Books have been written in an attempt to establish appropriate assumptions about borrowing rates: there is no attempt here to add to the literature, since it is of limited significance to the accounting matters that this chapter seeks to address. The most obvious, and perhaps most sensible, approach is to choose a rate which approximates to that which the importer would have to pay to obtain finance in that currency for that period covered by the debt obligations. That this will almost certainly lead to a recognition of interest expense at a different rate from that inherent in the actual discounting by the forfaiter, and thus a mismatch between the importer's interest charges in any period and the forfaiter's interest income for that period, does not matter. Of course, if the importer does know the rate of interest inherent in the bills or notes he will have to pay, that rate is the appropriate one to use, since it does indeed represent the actual cost of his credit.

Once the rate is established, the importer's total liability needs to be split between the cost of the goods or services purchased and the interest. The interest element will be debited to a balance sheet suspense account and amortised to interest expense in amounts proportionate to the outstanding 'cost of goods' element. The following is a simple example. Bills of exchange totalling £1,550,000 are payable over five years in four equal annual instalments of £300,000, plus a final payment of £350,000, and the importer's borrowing rate is assumed to be $16\frac{1}{2}\%$, compounded annually. From this information, the importer will calculate the implicit cost of the goods and the interest element in the total sum to be paid and spread these amounts over the period to the maturity of the final bill. The resulting figures are shown in Table 9.1.

Table 9.1   *Accounting by the importer: the debt obligation split between cost of goods and interest*

Time (years)	Total outstanding (£000s)	Cost of goods (£000s)	Rate of interest	Interest (£000s)	Cost repaid (£000s)	Total repaid (£000s)
0	1,550	994				
1	1,250	858	$16\frac{1}{2}\%$	164*	136	300
2	950	700	$16\frac{1}{2}\%$	142*	158	300
3	650	515	$16\frac{1}{2}\%$	115	185	300
4	350	300	$16\frac{1}{2}\%$	85	215	300
5	Nil	Nil	$16\frac{1}{2}\%$	50	300	350
				556	994	1,550

* $16\frac{1}{2}\% \times £994,000 = £164,000$; $16\frac{1}{2}\% \times £858,000 = £142,000$; etc.

The importer's accounting entries, year by year, are therefore as follows:

Àt time 0, that is, upon the receipt of the goods,

Dr. Inventory   £994,000
Dr. Interest suspense 556,000
Cr. Bills payable   1,550,000.

During Year 1, accounting period by accounting period, probably monthly,

Dr. Interest expense £164,000
Cr. Interest suspense 164,000.

At the end of Year 1, when the first bill matures,

Dr. Bills payable   £300,000
Cr. Cash   300,000.

Similar entries, following the figures in Table 9.1, need to be made until the last bill matures. The most significant point here is, again, that the importer should take care to ensure that he allocates his costs appropriately, since failure to do so will lead to distortion of his reported trading margins and financing costs. The calculation exemplified in Table 9.1 is seldom particularly difficult to perform with discount tables and even the most basic pocket calculator, since the cost of goods figure merely represents the present value of the future bill payments discounted at the appropriate interest rate.

In most circumstances, the outstanding debts in each currency will be translated into the importer's reporting currency and incorporated into his balance sheet at the spot rate of exchange each time accounts, for example monthly management accounts, are prepared. Obviously, any forward currency transaction hedging these debts should also be translated at the spot rate and any profit or loss inherent in them included in the accounts, even though the forward contracts themselves are contingent items rather than actual assets or liabilities.

Accounting by the forfaiter

A forfaiter may have to account for three separate financial items arising from any deal: option and commitment fees, the paper purchased, held and sold, and the funding he obtains for his purchase.

Fees

The accounting treatment appropriate for option and commitment fees mirrors that recommended above for those fees in the books of the payer, the exporter. In summary, an option fee should be credited in total to the forfaiter's fee income account as soon as he grants the option: if the fee is not receivable immediately, it should be accrued in total at that point. A commitment fee should be credited to a balance sheet suspense account and amortised to the forfaiter's fee income account over the commitment period, in amounts proportionate to the outstanding commitment (since the total commitment may be drawn down in instalments by the exporter). Any commitment fee not immediately receivable but chargeable immediately should be accrued.

Some accountants would argue that, on the grounds of prudence, no option or commitment fee should be credited in the forfaiter's accounts until it is actually received, or at least until its receipt is due, but there is seldom any question as to the validity of such fees and an exporter seldom alienates a forfaiter by an unjustified refusal to pay. Where, therefore, there is written confirmation of the granting of an option or a commitment and unless there is some reason to suppose that the exporter will refuse to pay, such caution is excessive and the fees should be accrued. In practice, of course, a forfaiter may well choose not to account for fees until their receipt is due or, even, until the fees are received, simply because the amounts involved are immaterial to his accounts. A forfaiter adopting this approach may find that his auditors disapprove, unless they believe that it represents an acceptable degree of prudence.

À forfait paper purchased and held

Accounting for the discount

When a forfaiter buys a debt obligation, he does so at a discount, the benefit of which he will gain upon the repayment of the debt itself. There are those, therefore, who maintain that this benefit should not be accounted for until the debt is repaid. To most, such an approach is unnecessarily cautious and unacceptable as a principle, since it leads to a mismatch of income and expense in the forfaiter's books as the forfaiter's borrowing costs – interest – will be accounted for over time.

The discount should, therefore, be spread over the period from the purchase of the paper to its maturity, at a rate which gives a constant return upon the amounts outstanding. To put it another way, the gross yield on the asset should not change while it is held. As explained in Chapter 6, the forfaiter will have determined the yield he wants from the paper before buying it and will have calculated the discount accordingly: in doing so, he will have compounded that yield annually or, more usually, semi-annually. Consequently, allocating the discount between accounting periods and making appropriate accruals in the accounts is a straightforward process.

As an illustration, the example in the previous section ('Accounting by the importer') can be used with the additional assumption that the forfaiter has purchased the bills of exchange at a discount to yield $16\frac{1}{2}\%$ compounded annually. (The yield need not be the same as the borrowing rate assumed in his calculations for accounting purposes by the importer. Indeed, it may well not be. It is in this case, for the sake of simplicity.) The forfaiter will therefore have paid the exporter £994,000, as shown in Table 9.2. The total discount is £556,000, which is spread between the individual bills and over the periods to maturity as Table 9.2 shows.

Table 9.2   À forfait paper purchased and held: accounting for the discount

Bill no.	Years to maturity	Purchase price (£000s)	Year 1 (£000s)	Discount taken to income					Maturity proceeds (£000s)
				Year 2 (£000s)	Year 3 (£000s)	Year 4 (£000s)	Year 5 (£000s)		
1	1	257	43						300
2	2	221	36	43					300
3	3	190	31	36	43				300
4	4	163	27	31	36	43			300
5	5	163	27	32	36	42	50		350
		994	164	142	115	85	50		1,550

Each year, the discount taken to income by the forfaiter represents the same yield on the cost plus discount already amortised of the outstanding bills. Thus, $16\frac{1}{2}\% \times 994 = 164$, the discount taken in Year 1. In Year 2, $16\frac{1}{2}\% \times (994 - 300 + 164) = 142$, the amount taken. By the same token, each bill provides a constant annual yield throughout its life. Thus, $16\frac{1}{2}\% \times 190 = 31$; $16\frac{1}{2}\% \times (190 + 31) = 36$; $16\frac{1}{2}\% \times (190 + 31 + 36) = 43$. Naturally, Table 9.2 could be greatly extended to show monthly allocations of income for the period, in which case those monthly allocations for any one bill in any year would be equal in this illustration but would, for example, be larger in the second half of the year than the first if the yield were compounded semi-annually rather than annually as here: in other words, the figure upon which the yield is earned would change not annually but every six months.

The forfaiter's accounting entries are as follows. Upon purchase of the paper,

Dr. Bills purchased   £994,000
Cr. Cash   994,000.

In Year 1, probably month by month,

Dr. Amortised discount (Asset account)   £164,000
Cr. Discount earned (Income account)   164,000.

At the end of Year 1, when the first bill matures,

Dr. Cash   £300,000
Cr. Bills purchased   257,000
Cr. Amortised discount   43,000.

Similar entries, following the figures in Table 9.2, need to be made until the last bill is repaid.

Accounting for investment paper versus accounting for trading paper

Whether the forfaiter is acting in the primary or secondary market, that is, buying from an exporter or another forfaiter, the process above will be necessary.

It is applicable, too, whether the forfaiter is buying the paper with the intention of holding it to maturity, that is, as an investment, or of trading it. However, the question of intent at the date of purchase is significant for accounting purposes as it may have a bearing upon the value at which the paper is held in the accounts (its carrying value).

The basic point is this. If an asset is held as an investment, then its market value at any moment is not significant unless any fall below its carrying value represents a permanent diminution in value. The logic is that an investment will be held until any temporary drop is recovered. (Needless to say, accounting convention seldom permits any write-up in carrying value, however permanent such a surplus may seem, as this is deemed imprudent.) If, on the other hand, an asset is held for trading purposes, then its carrying value must be the lower of cost (in the case of forfaited paper, original cost plus discount amortised to date) and current market value.

An increase in interest rates since forfaited paper was purchased, therefore, does not affect the maturity value of the paper and thus cannot of itself justify a reduction in the carrying value of investment paper, but it may well require a reduction in the carrying value of trading paper, since it will reduce the price at which it can be resold. However, the absence of any formal market-place in which à forfait paper is traded often makes the assessment of market value difficult, so that any interest-rate increase will have to be large and apparently likely to be held before anyone insists on a write-down for that reason. There is another point here, too. Any increase in rates which appears permanent and is so substantial that paper the funding of which is not precisely matched with low fixed-rate borrowing starts to show a negative margin will require a provision against future losses from that paper, in addition to any write-down in the carrying value itself – and this applies as much to investment paper as to trading paper.

The next question which arises in this regard is whether assets should be treated for write-down purposes or for the purposes of a future losses provision individually or within classes. Since accounting convention will not, as stated above, countenance writing-up the carrying value of assets, treating them individually is more conservative than looking at classes of assets as the latter may harbour some assets the market values of which are higher than their carrying value and the surpluses of which will offset the deficits on others. Because any forfaiter will tend to look upon his paper as a portfolio (or as an investment portfolio and a trading portfolio), treating them individually must also be less realistic. Identifiable groups of forfaited assets (for example, assets in particular currencies or representing particular sovereign risks) in each of his portfolios should be reviewed periodically by the forfaiter who should then make any appropriate write-downs and loss provisions. If he does not do this, it is likely that his auditors will.

Bad debt provisions

The other provision which a forfaiter may require, whether against investment paper or trading paper, is a non-payment provision. As in the case of any international lender, this can arise from the failure of the borrower (in the case of à forfait finance, this will usually be the guarantor) or from sovereign risk. In either case, the necessity for a provision will often become apparent long before the payment date of any particular bill or note arrives: perhaps other bills or notes in the series are dishonoured, perhaps the guarantor signals his intention not to pay for one reason or another, perhaps a national debt crisis arises in the country from which payment is due, or perhaps other forfaiters and lenders suffer non-payment of amounts due to them. Whatever the reason, as soon as the forfaiter has cause to doubt the eventual or even timely payment of amounts due to him, he must determine and set up an appropriate specific provision immediately. This banal statement obscures the real difficulty which often attends this judgemental process.

In this book, it is possible only to outline certain guidelines for making the judgement. First, it is sensible to err on the side of caution. Second, it is very unusual in forfaiting for a financially viable guarantor not to pay up in the end, since his reputation would probably otherwise suffer. Third, financially distressed guarantors are extremely rare in à forfait finance. Fourth, even where the forfaiter has no real doubts that he will eventually receive his money, there may be a case for a provision against legal costs, financing costs while the debt is overdue (though the guarantor will usually make at least a token payment for this), or both. Fifth, it is instructive to discover the actions taken with regard to provisions by other lenders similarly afflicted: indeed, auditors will tend to advocate and even commend a consistent approach. Sixth, an arbitrary percentage of the amount outstanding is an unsatisfactory basis for any provision and even more so when it is merely a device for spreading a known need for a 100% provision over a number of years.

Seventh, sovereign risk is, almost by definition, all or nothing. As a result, popular though it has become in recent years, particularly with auditors, to set a percentage provision against specific perceived sovereign risks, it is very difficult to see any justification for this approach, as a country can be expected to pay either none of its debt or all of it, even though its repayment may be rescheduled. No significant sovereign default in recent times has not been followed by agreement of eventual payment along with appropriate interest thereon. As a rule of thumb, therefore, it is very hard to find adequate justification for a sovereign loan loss provision *per se*, and impossible to justify a partial sovereign loan loss provision. Of course, a provision against legal or financing costs may, as stated above, be appropriate where sovereign problems are involved.

Essentially, the above comments about non-payment provisions apply to specific debts. In addition to such specific provisions, however, lenders often set up general provisions. The basic justification for these is that there are debts in the balance sheet which are already bad, even though the lender does not yet know it. The amount to be set aside may be determined by reference to experience. For example, $X\%$ of turnover or average debt on the books during the year or in the past N years has eventually been written off and therefore total provisions of $X\%$ are needed at the end of every year: specific provisions of $Y\%$ have already been set up and therefore a general provision of $(X\% - Y\%)$ is required. In strict accounting terms, a general provision set up on this basis may, indeed, be justified.

Unfortunately, general provisions are often set up arbitrarily and depend more upon the profitability of the company than upon the needs of the business. In other cases, the above 'scientific' approach may be finessed by increasing or decreasing the amount so calculated by a figure which is justified by obscure reference to 'changes in market conditions', 'changes in world conditions' or 'changes in the nature or conduct of the business'.

Such cynicism leaves the whole notion of 'general provisions' open to doubt. It is scarcely surprising, therefore, that many forfaiters do not set up general provisions for bad debts and that their auditors concur.

À forfait paper sold

When a primary or secondary market forfaiter sells forfaited paper, the sale proceeds will need to be compared with its original cost to the forfaiter plus any discount amortised to the date of sale less any provisions set up specifically against it. These 'carrying cost' elements will need to be removed from the books of account and the difference between their total and the sale proceeds represents a profit or a loss which should, in all cases, be credited or debited to an appropriate income statement account.

There is no accounting principle which would permit deferring the recognition of a loss on a sale. As noted in Chapter 1, forfaiters in recent times have occasionally sold à forfait paper on a variable interest-rate basis. In such a case, the sale proceeds are open to variation in the future depending upon interest-rate movements. Therefore, the seller might regard it as prudent not to recognise an apparent profit on the initial sale but to defer it until the final interest-rate reassessment in case future reassessments result in a repayment to the buyer. In fact, the uncertainties surrounding such a transaction are generally such that any repayments may exceed the initial profit so that the amount deferred is inadequate as a provision: alternatively, it may never be needed and is therefore wholly excessive. In either case, the deferral of the initial profit cannot be justified on the grounds of any accounting principle, not even prudence, and so should be avoided: it is inappropriate to make a provision where the amount needed is incapable of assessment.

Funding

Accounting for a forfaiter's borrowings is precisely that adopted by any borrower. The debits and credits upon the receipt of the loan and its repayment are self-evident and need not be discussed here. Similarly, accounting for the related interest cost is simple. The only point to be made is that interest must be accrued and not simply debited to financing costs upon its payment.

As noted in Chapter 8, however, the forfaiter's funding may not be quite as straightforward as taking a loan in the same currency as that in which the paper purchased is denominated. He may borrow in a different currency, either because borrowing in the paper's currency is difficult or, more likely, because another currency provides, in his judgement, better terms even taking into account likely foreign currency swap costs. Borrowing, for example, in Deutschmarks and lending in US dollars entails a spot foreign exchange contract to change the Deutschmarks into US dollars. This gives the forfaiter an open US dollar long position, that is, a net asset in US dollars, and an open Deutschmark short position or net Deutschmark liability. The forfaiter must revalue each of these positions into his reporting currency at spot rates of exchange. Doing so will yield at any time a gain or a loss and this must be taken to the forfaiter's income statement immediately: there is no accounting justification for any deferral.

The forfaiter may, however, choose to cover his exposed asset and liability positions by entering into forward foreign exchange contracts to sell US dollars and buy Deutschmarks. Provided that the maturity dates of the borrowing and the assets it is funding are very closely matched, he will have

Table 9.3   The forfaiter's balance sheets before and after a change in spot currency rates

US$ = DM3

Forfait paper	$1,000,000	Borrowing	$1,000,000
Deferred swap loss	16,667	Value of forward contracts	16,667 (1)
	$1,016,667		$1,016,667

(1) Sell forward DM2,950,000 at
    Buy forward
    $1 = DM3 — $1,000,000
    983,333
    Net liability $ 16,667

(2) Sell forward DM2,950,000 at
    Buy forward
    $1 = DM2.8 — $1,000,000
    1,053,571
    Net asset $ 53,571

US$ = DM2.8

Forfait paper	$1,000,000	Borrowing	$1,071,428
Deferred swap loss	16,667 (4)		
Value of forward contracts	53,571 (2)		
Loss on swap costs	1,190 (3)		
	$1,071,428		$1,071,428

(3) DM50,000 at $1 = DM3   16,667
    DM50,000 at $1 = DM2.8   17,857
    Loss $ 1,190

(4) To be debited to financing costs in equal instalments over 6 months

a 'pure' swap. The net profit or loss inherent in the swap itself is known at the outset. It can therefore be spread, as an element in the cost of financing the transactions, over its life. Provided that the asset and liability and the forward currency contract itself are all translated into the forfaiter's reporting currency at spot rates, the gain or loss on the asset and liability will be offset by a loss or gain on the forward contract so that no distortions occur in the forfaiter's funding costs.

For example, the forfaiter buys an asset for US\$1 million and borrows DM 3 million. Spot currency rates are US\$1 = DM3. The forfaiter's reporting currency is US dollars. The asset and the liability mature six months hence. He swaps DM3 million for US\$1 million spot in order to buy the paper and contracts six months forward to sell US\$1 million for DM2,950,000, thereby selling the repayment proceeds of the asset for approximately the sum needed to repay his borrowing. The loss on these transactions, no matter how currency parities move in the meantime, is DM50,000. Since Deutschmark interest rates are generally lower than US dollar rates, he will have funded his higher-yielding US dollar assets with lower-cost borrowing, and the DM50,000 is, in effect, an additional financing cost of doing this. It should therefore be spread over the six months' life of the transactions just as though it were interest. Assume that immediately the transaction has been done, spot currency rates change to US\$1 = DM2.8. The forfaiter's balance sheets before and after the change in rates following the above accounting and revaluation rules are as shown in Table 9.3.

The forfaiter's profit and loss account arising simply from the change in rates is as follows.

Loss on borrowing \$1,071,428 − \$1,000,000 = \$71,428
Gain in value of forward contracts
$$\$53,571 + \$16,667 = \quad 70,238$$

Net loss arising because spot sale of
DM(3,000,000) exceeds forward purchase
of DM(2,950,000)   = \$1,190

In practice, as observed in Chapter 8, a forfaiter will generally not cover net asset and liability currency positions in this way. Any swap transactions will tend to be 'impure', that is, the forward currency transactions will not mature at the same time as both the assets and the liabilities: indeed, since forfaiters do not generally match their funding to their paper in terms of maturity dates, 'pure' swaps are not possible. Very often, forward currency transactions will bear little obvious relation in terms of maturity dates to either the assets or the liabilities they ostensibly hedge, since the forfaiter's principal objective is to cover his overall positions rather than his specific maturities. In addition, of course, the forfaiter's currency assets and liabilities include amortised discount and accrued interest which are very seldom matched by forward currency transactions even though they have specific and identifiable maturity dates in the same way as the assets and liabilities which give rise to them.

Consequently, any review of the forfaiter's assets and liabilities and forward currency contracts will give the impression that the forward contracts are not purely hedging mechanisms. In so far as accounting literature will therefore classify them as 'speculative' contracts, there is an argument that they should be revalued at forward rates to cover the period when the forfaiter prepares accounts. Since, however, forfaiters are seldom traders in foreign currency simply for speculative reasons, this treatment defies common sense. It appears more appropriate to revalue all forward currency contracts at spot rates, since these are the rates at which the assets and liabilities to which they are in reality related will also be translated.

The most important point is that forward currency contracts must be revalued when the forfaiter prepares accounts and their net value included in his balance sheet with an appropriate debit or credit to his income statement, generally to an account quite separate from amortised discount, à forfait trading profits or losses or financing costs, since it is very hard to relate such currency profits or losses specifically to any à forfait trading or financing decision.

Accounting for the grace period

Accounting for the grace period seldom causes any difficulties. Since it is merely an extension of the period assumed in the discounting process from the date of purchase of the forfaited assets to their maturity, the slightly larger discount arising from it will be spread over a slightly longer period. If repayment of the assets in fact takes place before the end of the grace period, then there will be a minor additional credit to income to be taken at the date of repayment which otherwise would be spread over the remaining, usually very short,time.

However, as noted in Chapter 5, there are occasional disputes as to the period of grace to be assumed. Methods of solving such disagreements can produce contingent and deferred balance sheet items. Adequate reference to these is made in Chapter 5 and no further comments are needed here.

Accounting by the guarantor

A guarantor of an à forfait transaction has two separate financial items to account for, the guarantee fee and settlement of the debt obligation itself.

The guarantee fee

The accounting treatment appropriate to the guarantee fee mirrors that which, as stated above, should be adopted by its payer, the importer. In short, a guarantee fee should be credited to a balance sheet suspense account by the guarantor and spread over the period during which the guarantee is provided in amounts proportionate to the face value of the bills or notes outstanding. Any guarantee fee due but not charged should be accrued. Because of its probable immateriality to his accounts, a guarantor may well, in practice, credit the fee directly in total to his income statement when he charges it or, even, when it is paid, although this is not good accounting practice.

Settlement of the debt obligation

Once a bill or note is due for repayment, the guarantor needs to remove its face value from his commitment records and incorporate it in his balance sheet. Because payment to the forfaiter and receipt of the same amount are due simultaneously, the only balance sheet entries that need to be made are Dr. Cash received and Cr. Cash paid. However, since there is the possibility that receipt or payment will not be timely, the entries may be Dr. Amounts due for bills, Cr. Amounts payable on bills, with appropriate reversing and cash entries when settlement takes place. This second approach has the merit that it highlights amounts overdue.

Commitment records

Exporter

The exporter will naturally require a record of those à forfait transactions to which he is committed and those upon which he has an option in order to ensure that requirements concerning documentation and delivery of documents are satisfied at the appropriate time, to ensure that he receives payment in accordance with the terms of the à forfait agreement, and to check requests for option and commitment fees from the forfaiter as well as their appropriate accrual. Similarly, he will require an accurate list of his forward foreign currency commitments.

In addition, the exporter is well advised to maintain a record of à forfait transactions once he has received payment but the bills or notes involved have still not matured. This is a sensible precaution, since, as noted in Chapter 4, the exporter still has some risk, albeit very small, arising from the transaction. Such a record should be in maturity date order and should be regularly reviewed to ensure that the exporter is up to date with any developments, for example, sovereign default problems or legal cases concerning an obligor's duties, which might have an impact on his liabilities.

Importer

As soon as he has been charged for the goods or services which are the subject of the forfaiting transaction, an importer will have an automatic record of his payment commitments in his balance sheet. Separate commitment records, therefore, are necessary only in the period between his acceptance of the finance terms which include the forfaiting transaction and the entry of the purchase in his accounts. They are necessary in order that the importer records his cash-flow commitments together with any related financing that he has arranged and the consequent reduction in his undrawn finance facilities. Naturally, it is important that such commitment records be kept under review to ensure their accuracy and, in particular, that purchases which have been recorded in the balance sheet have been removed from the commitment records. This will be facilitated by keeping them in the order in which the goods or services are expected to be delivered.

Of course, the importer must also maintain an accurate list of those forward foreign currency contracts to which he is committed.

Forfaiter

The forfaiter will need a list of options he has extended and a list of commitments to which he is bound and will need to ensure that the details thereon are appropriately incorporated in the management reports outlined in Chapter 8. These lists serve a further purpose: they assist in the timely request of exporters for option and commitment fees. They must be regularly reviewed for accuracy, in particular to ensure that expired options, options that have become commitments and commitments that have become actual à forfait transactions have been correctly removed, and also to ensure that option and commitment fees have been properly accrued.

Naturally, the forfaiter also needs an accurate list of forward foreign currency contracts to which he is committed.

Guarantor

The guarantor's contingent assets and liabilities need to be recorded accurately throughout the guarantee period. In addition, the guarantor needs a list of those guarantees he has indicated his willingness to provide, even though the relevant trade transaction has not yet taken place – in other words, guarantees supporting forfaiters' commitments. This is important to ensure that the guarantor's customer, the importer, does not exceed predetermined finance facility limits in obtaining further guarantees or credit from the guarantor before he actually signs the guarantee or aval to which he is committed. As always, all commitment lists, which have the added benefit of assisting in the appropriate and timely requests for and accrual of guarantee fees, should be reviewed regularly to determine their accuracy.

Settlement records

All participants in à forfait transactions should, as already emphasised, maintain accurate records by maturity date of outstanding paper. In the case of the forfaiter and the guarantor, it is particularly important that such settlement records should be the specific responsibility of that employee designated to request payment of the paper at the appropriate time and to forward the paper for collection of money from the payer (the guarantor in the case of the forfaiter and the importer in the case of the guarantor). Items overdue for settlement must be reported to top management immediately.

Taxation

The general rules of taxation which apply to any trading or financial transaction apply equally to à forfait transactions. In the United Kingdom, therefore, the Inland Revenue will generally tax fees and any gain or loss on the sale of à forfait paper as well as specific valuation provisions (that is, write-downs to mark value of specific assets) on the basis upon which they are reflected in the accounts: this follows the principle, adopted by the tax authorities, whereby the accounting treatment of a transaction is certainly a useful indicator of the appropriate tax treatment for it, even if not the final determinant.

The accounting treatment, however, is irrelevant to the taxation of general bad debt provisions. Whereas default by a debtor is usually sufficient reason for the tax allowability of a specific bad debt provision, a general provision, by its nature, is unsupportable by reference to any particular debtor's default. Consequently, the Inland Revenue will not allow general provisions against tax. Provisions for anticipated future losses on specific assets are also unlikely to be allowed on the not unreasonable ground that such provisions are estimates and cannot therefore be 'proven'.

Interest receivable and payable on term borrowing is also treated differently for tax purposes and accounting purposes. The Inland Revenue tax such interest on a 'paid' and not an 'accrual' basis. Again, this is the same approach as they adopt towards any trading or financial company. The principle here is that it is inequitable to charge or allow an item for tax purposes if the related cash has not changed hands. By the same token, it has been established by a House of Lords decision in *Willingale* v. *International Commercial Bank* (1978) that discount on forfaited assets is not generally taxable until it is received, even though the forfaiter amortises it over the period from purchase to maturity. It is uncertain to what extent the Inland Revenue are prepared to accept that this decision applies to all à forfait paper, since International Commercial Bank was demonstrably an end-investor in forfaited paper and not a trader.

It certainly applies to pure investors, it probably applies to the investment portfolio of a forfaiter who both invests and trades, but it may not apply to trading paper, although the actual period the paper is held rather than its categorisation as 'investment' or 'trading' paper by the forfaiter may determine its tax treatment. Similarly, an importer, amortising the discount or interest he is paying on any debt obligation, will probably not find it allowed for tax purposes until it is paid, that is, until the paper matures: in that the transaction is analogous, from the point of view of the importer, to a medium-term loan, this is not surprising, since, as stated above, interest on term borrowing is treated as allowable when paid.

In all tax matters, of course, it is difficult to generalise about individual cases. Tax treatment is open to discussion, and sometimes to negotiation, between the taxpayer and the tax authorities. This is particularly true in respect of the taxability and tax allowability of the discount on à forfait paper.

10

Notable cases in
à forfait finance

As indicated earlier in this book, particularly in Chapter 4, there have been
very few legal decisions affecting the à forfait markets, primary or
secondary. However, there have been instances of disputes between the
various parties to an à forfait transaction which have been settled out of
court. In so far as these cases have become public knowledge and to the
extent that any general points of law, or, indeed, common sense, can be
gleaned from them, they are outlined here. Because of their controversial
nature and the fact that no legal decisions were delivered in respect of them,
the names of the parties involved have been changed: in addition, for ease of
assimilation, the facts of the cases have been simplified.

Turbines or not turbines?

In this case, a Swiss manufacturing company, here referred to as 'Turbo',
contracted to sell turbines to a company, here referred to as 'Buyer', situated
elsewhere in Europe, let us say in Ruritania. The two companies and their
management personnel were well known to one another after several years
of mutually profitable business relations. This contract, involving over
US$4,000,000, promised to be equally beneficial, particularly to Turbo,
who had been suffering the effects of recession and needed the business to
ease an uncomfortable cash position.

The first snag arose quite early in the negotiations when Buyer made it
clear that the size of the contract meant that they needed credit. Having
already tried locally to obtain the foreign currency finance needed for the
deal, they had established that it was available only at unsatisfactorily high
rates of interest because of its medium-term nature. Turbo were, needless to
say, perturbed by this news because they needed payment sooner rather

than later: indeed, they would have liked pre-shipment finance, if possible, but, if not, payment as soon as delivery took place.

Turbo turned to their principal bankers, here referred to as 'All-finance', for advice. All-finance sugested à forfait finance and explained in some detail how it worked as Turbo had never used this method of finance before. Turbo liked the general concept though they made it plain that they would need to approach Buyer on the subject and, in particular, that they would have to gain an assurance from Buyer that an acceptable bank guarantor could be found for the bills of exchange which they envisaged would be used as the debt instruments. All-finance, meanwhile, decided that they wanted to sell the paper on the secondary market and set about finding buyers. Within a short time, Buyer had obtained the agreement of a first-class Ruritanian bank, 'Ruribank', to act as guarantor, and Turbo and All-finance had agreed the terms of the discount to be applied to the bills of exchange. Turbo had drawn up the bills and All-finance had found three secondary forfaiters, who, between them, were prepared to purchase all the bills, a series of eight notes of over US$500,000 each, payable at six-monthly intervals, the first due six months after shipment of the turbines.

Shortly before delivery of the turbines was due, Buyer signed the bills and the account officer with whom they had dealt at Ruribank, 'Mr Signor', signed the letter of guarantee on behalf of the bank. These documents were lodged with another of Turbo's banks. Once evidence of delivery of the turbines was to hand, this bank released the documents, appropriately dated, to Turbo, who presented them to All-finance. They were immediately discounted and simultaneously sold on to the secondary forfaiters. All had gone like clockwork and all parties to the transaction were well-satisfied.

This happy state of affairs did not last long. The turbines had a basic design fault. Even worse, before the first bill of exchange was due for repayment, Turbo lost a major case in the United States and they were told to pay damages far exceeding their net assets: even the proceeds from discounting Buyer's debt obligations could not overcome this disaster. Turbo were bankrupt. Naturally, Turbo were in no position to rectify Buyer's faulty turbines.

At maturity, Buyer refused to settle their obligations under the first maturing bill of exchange. Worse, from the forfaiters' standpoint, so did Ruribank on the grounds, apart from any others, that the guarantee itself was not valid, since Mr Signor alone did not have the authority to bind the bank in such sums, and that any guarantee, under the laws of Ruritania, was revocable at any time until its beneficiary made a formal claim under it unless it was expressed as being irrevocable: this guarantee was not.

The further the forfaiters' lawyers looked into the case, the more difficult it became. Apart from the other problems, it transpired that Ruritanian law required bills of exchange to be drawn up on particular documents issued by the state which facilitated the collection of stamp duty: such forms had not been used. Not only this, but the permission of the Central Bank of Ruritania was required for any Ruritanian company to bind itself to remit foreign currency overseas: no such permission had been sought.

What was the position of each of the parties in this drama?

The secondary forfaiters

The secondary forfaiters had purchased the bills without recourse to All-finance. They had assumed that any default by Buyer arising from a dispute as to the satisfactory completion of the underlying trade contract was irrelevant to their position, since the guarantee by Ruribank was an abstract obligation giving Ruribank the absolute duty to pay. The first step then was to make a formal demand for payment from Ruribank or, failing this, from Buyer. The demand had to be made in accordance with the laws of Ruritania, since this was where the bills were to be presented.

These laws stipulated that anyone formally protesting against the dishonour of a bill of exchange had to do so via a notary public and the document evidencing this had to be registered with the appropriate section of the Ministry of Trade. These were not onerous obligations in themselves but did carry the cost of the notary public's fees and, more significant, an administrative fee of $\frac{1}{2}\%$ of the face value of the bill. In addition, of course, every day that passed beyond the maturity date of the bill cost the forfaiters interest on the overdue debt.

Despite these costs, there was no alternative to this formal protest: although the secondary forfaiters' lawyers felt that Ruribank's refusal to pay did not constitute a formal revocation of the bill, such formal revocation might come at any time and protesting against the dishonour, which represented a formal claim on the guarantee, was the only means under Ruritanian law by which it could be avoided.

This, however, by no means ensured that Ruribank would be forced to pay. As noted earlier, any guarantor may be able to avoid his obligation if the guarantee is not itself valid. If Ruribank were able to substantiate the claim that Mr Signor had exceeded his authority, then the guarantee would, indeed, probably be invalid.

In these circumstances, the secondary forfaiters could seek redress against Buyer, who, they similarly thought, had an absolute obligation to pay under the abstract bill of exchange. Unfortunately, they again had a problem in pursuing this argument because the bill was itself formally invalid, since it did not conform to the Ruritanian documentary re-quirements and, anyhow, a Ruritanian court would be likely to throw it out because no permission to transfer foreign currency had been obtained. Even if equity prevailed over these difficulties and Buyer did agree to pay, the absence of exchange control permission would probably render such an agreement worthless: the money might well not get beyond the state authorities. In that unhappy event, Buyer would have discharged their responsibilities but the secondary forfaiters would be out of pocket with no obvious legal means of redress.

However, the secondary forfaiters might have more success in demanding redress from All-finance since, as stated in Chapter 4, the primary forfaiter has a duty to sell valid documents. If Ruritanian courts declared the bill invalid then, prima facie, All-finance had not fulfilled this duty.

All-finance

All-finance soon found itself in the firing line. There was no easy defence to the contention that it had not sold valid bills, validly guaranteed. It sought immediately to rely upon the 'non-recourse' clause in the bill of exchange. Unsurprisingly, All-finance's lawyers did not think this much of a defence, since, as stated in Chapter 4, the seller of a bill of exchange cannot absolve himself of all responsibilities by the use of such a clause. Failing this, All-finance claimed that the secondary forfaiters had a responsibility to check the documentation in the transaction for validity and could not expect to rely upon All-finance to do so. This defence, too, is shaky, following the arguments as to the particular duties of the primary forfaiter outlined in Chapter 4: even if the secondary forfaiters had all the details of the transaction, including the names of the importer and exporter, à forfait market practice would not expect them to have to perform these checks themselves.

The only potentially fruitful line of approach for All-finance was a claim against Turbo. If All-finance had a duty to sell valid bills, validly guaranteed, then so did Turbo.

Turbo

Turbo would undoubtedly seek to rely on the non-recourse clause as absolving them of the duty to sell valid bills, validly guaranteed. Their likelihood of succeeding with such a defence would, perhaps, have been marginally better than that of All-finance if they were able to demonstrate that, given their inexperience in forfaiting, it was unreasonable to expect them to perform the detailed checks necessary to prove the validity of the documents. In other words, if Turbo could persuade the courts that their duties had been assumed by All-finance, they might succeed in avoiding liability.

There was unlikely to be documentary evidence to back up such an argument, but market practice would certainly tend to show that an exporter relies upon the forfaiter's expertise in matters such as formal documentation and legal requirements in the importer's country. However, it is by no means certain that market practice is a sufficient justification for negligent disregard of one's duties and, if there was no evidence that Turbo had ever discussed or even considered these questions, the defence was highly suspect.

In fact, of course, Turbo were never called upon to defend themselves. All-finance recognised the futility of proceeding against a company rapidly proceeding into liquidation. This emphasises one other point. It had not occurred to All-finance to check the credit-worthiness of Turbo when the original request for finance was made. All-finance did, of course, ensure that Ruribank were credit-worthy and ran a cursory check on Buyer, but assumed that they would never have to make any claim on the exporter.

What if the security had been an aval rather than a separate guarantee? This would have made little difference to the arguments. Ruribank would still have been able to walk away from their obligations if Mr Signor had been its sole signatory. Further, the aval would have been invalid at the outset because the bill of exchange did not conform to local legal requirements and was therefore itself invalid.

Bring on the cranes

In the case above, the facts and chronological order of events as well as the arguments advanced are set out in some detail. To avoid repetition, the approach in this second case is varied so that details are kept to a minimum and, instead, some of the points brought out in Chapter 4 are related specifically to the litigation.

In this case, a primary forfaiter, an English finance company, called here 'Primary Finance', sold bills of exchange to a secondary market purchaser 'Middleman' who, in turn, resold them to four other secondary market traders who will be known here collectively as 'Four-in-Hand'. The bills were thought to have been issued in respect of an export transaction (of cranes from West Germany to the United Arab Emirates) but it turned out that this was not the case. There was, in fact, no exporter. The bills related to a financial transaction, that is to say the 'importer' was not buying cranes at all but using the bills in order to raise funds to reduce its own borrowings.

The bills were dishonoured, the guaranteeing bank did not pay and litigation followed. The sale of the bills to Middleman by Primary and the sale of the bills by Middleman to Four-in-Hand were expressed to be without recourse. Additionally, two of the purchasers from Middleman had imposed reserves, one reserve relating to receipt of satisfactory documentation, the other being that Middleman had satisfied himself that the obligations of the 'importer' and the guaranteeing bank were valid and binding.

The type of paper in which the forfaiting market deals, the differing obligations of the seller in the primary and secondary markets, the meaning of the words 'without recourse' and the ability of the purchaser to impose reserves were brought sharply into focus, as well as the question of which country or countries had jurisdiction over the case and which country's or countries' laws governed the transaction.

Before considering these specific points, however, it is worth making a general observation which supports the contention made elsewhere in this book that the à forfait market is distinguished by the simplicity of its documentation, a simplicity which nevertheless does not generally obscure the responsibilities of the parties to an à forfait transaction but which must be understood by those parties.

During the course of the case, it became apparent that, in dealings in the market, very little is committed to writing. Sometimes there was an offer telex giving some details about the transaction, such as the nature of the underlying trade. At other times, there was a telex merely accepting an oral offer and this had very little detail about the transaction itself in it, mainly concentrating upon settlement terms, for example, transfer of funds and settlement date. It was clear that the market moves quickly and there was a general consensus among the parties involved that it could not operate properly if it had to deal with bulky purchase and sale agreements relating to the bills themselves whenever a transaction took place. It is apparent that the market, notwithstanding litigation such as this, continues to work on the basis that it can properly make assumptions about the obligations which market practice dictates are taken on by the various parties to a transaction. Paperwork is thereby kept to a minimum but there always exists provision for the relevant party to make clear that those assumptions are not applicable in a particular case.

This raises the question of what constitutes generally accepted market practice. In the course of the litigation, it was necessary to explore market practice to see whether or not the parties to the transaction in contention had failed to comply with it. Evidence of the operations of the market that was gathered was pretty consistent. The case itself was settled on terms where Primary and the guaranteeing bank met the plaintiff's losses in full, exonerating Middleman entirely. A statement was read in open court to the effect that Middleman had acted in accordance with the best practice of the à forfait market. By contrast, it was implicitly accepted by Primary that it had not. These conclusions, and the actions which gave rise to them, have been used in the preparation of this book, so that the procedures and principles in its earlier chapters can be assumed to reflect accepted market practice.

As to the matters brought out by the case, they can be summarised as follows and tend to illustrate a number of the comments made in Chapter 4.

Jurisdiction and proper law appropriate to the case

No general comments can usefully be made here, since, as explained in Chapter 4, the question of jurisdiction and/or law appropriate to any particular à forfait transaction depends entirely upon the circumstances of the case itself. It is worth pointing out, however, that there was considerable debate amongst and within the various legal advisers as to where the case should be heard and which country's or countries' laws governed it. At various times, West Germany, the United Arab Emirates and England were canvassed as the appropriate countries: and it was thought for a time that Middleman would have a liability to Four-in-Hand under English law but would not be able to sue Primary successfully under West German law. There was no specific provision in the documents to the transaction relating to either the jurisdiction or to the proper law governing it. This never became a critical issue in the case, largely because it was settled before all the legal arguments were resolved. It is undoubtedly true, however, that such a provision would have expedited matters.

The type of paper involved in the transaction

As already stated, the purchasers in the secondary market were under the mistaken impression that they were buying trade-backed paper rather than the financial paper which the bills of exchange in fact represented. Indeed, Primary thought this, too. In Chapter 4, it was emphasised that the primary forfaiter is well advised both to establish the nature of the paper involved in an à forfait transaction and, when he is selling it on, to ensure that the buyer is informed if the paper is financial. If he fails to perform the second of these functions, then, because most paper in the à forfait market is trade-backed and because, in general, most forfaiters prefer trade-backed paper and, indeed, many refuse to trade in financial paper, the secondary market buyer would be entitled to assume that he was purchasing trade-backed paper.

It follows, therefore, that, from the standpoint of the secondary market buyer, the paper he bought was not what he could reasonably have expected it to be. He was, as a consequence, able to claim that he did not buy what he had a right to believe he was buying and that the primary forfaiter was obliged to take the paper back. The outcome of the case certainly implied that the primary forfaiter at least acknowledged that such a claim might succeed.

Difference between primary and secondary market obligations

Chapter 4 set out the different obligations of primary and secondary forfaiters and explained the practical and legal reasons for the differences. Following the arguments outlined there, Middleman could not be said to have had the same responsibilities as Primary. Were this not the case, Four-in-Hand might have been able to claim against Middleman who would not, in turn, have been able to pass the claim back to Primary. The fact was, however, that Middleman was not a primary forfaiter: he could not have been assumed by Primary to have the same obligations as those of a primary forfaiter but was entitled to rely upon Primary to provide appropriate information, and, specifically, to check the bona fides of the transaction and of the debt obligations. By the same token, Four-in-Hand, although one step further down the chain of purchase, were in the same effective position as Middleman.

Consequently, Four-in-Hand's claim lay against Primary via Middleman. The outcome of the case showed that the primary forfaiter probably felt that he might well eventually have to accept that his responsibilities were indeed more extensive than those of any subsequent purchaser and that he had failed to discharge them adequately.

The meaning of the words 'without recourse'

Despite all the above arguments that the primary forfaiter had not fulfilled his obligation to disclose, or even establish, the precise nature and bona fides of the transaction underlying the finance which the various forfaiters involved in the case were being asked to provide, and that this obligation was uniquely that of Primary to perform, the whole case against Primary and, indeed, any against Middleman would have fallen had the 'without recourse' clause on the bills of exchange been held to absolve the seller from any and every responsibility.

Although this matter did not actually proceed to a court judgement, it is again reasonable to infer from the settlement of the case that Primary did not feel that this would be an appropriate interpretation of the clause. The reasons for this conclusion were probably similar to those explained in Chapter 4. In short, the clause could not help him because he had not sold a valid claim arising from a bona fide transaction.

Imposition of 'reserves' by purchasers

Although Four-in-Hand sought to rely upon the reserves they had imposed at the time of their purchase of the bills of exchange from Middleman, the validity and practical usefulness of those reserves were, because of the early settlement of the case, never properly established. From an academic standpoint, this is unfortunate. It is, however, possible to hazard some suggestions.

The first reserve claimed the right of Four-in-Hand to reject the à forfait transaction if they did not receive satisfactory documentation. In practice, such a reserve would seem to have been entirely unnecessary, since, even had all the documentation of the transaction been satisfactory, Four-in-

Hand would have avoided loss by being able to rely upon the far more fundamental breaches of responsibility noted above.

The second reserve, if it could have been relied upon, would have enabled Four-in-Hand to reject the transaction if Middleman had not satisfied himself that the importer's obligations and those of the guarantor were valid and binding. In other words, Middleman was being required to accept duties which he, as a secondary forfaiter, did not normally have. A secondary forfaiter can frequently discharge duties of this sort only by relying upon the written word of the primary forfaiter. In these circumstances, therefore, Middleman's acceptance of the reserve and discharge of the obligations arising from it would be worth no more than the word of Primary: but Primary already had, as stated repeatedly above, the duty as the primary forfaiter to ensure these matters anyhow. Thus, again, it is hard to see how this reserve could have helped, since the onus would have fallen upon Primary via Middleman in any event.

If this analysis is correct, the moral seems to be that reserves, although extensively used by secondary forfaiters, are seldom of genuine value to them. They seem to be a placebo rather than a cure. It will generally be far more realistic for a secondary forfaiter to rely upon the general obligations placed upon the primary forfaiter than to seek to reinforce his position by the use of reserves.

What was the position of the guarantor?

It has been stressed in this book that an aval or guarantee, if it is to be used in an à forfait transaction, must be abstract, so that any dispute as to the underlying transaction is irrelevant to the guarantor's absolute duty to pay. If, however, the aval or guarantee is itself not valid, then it cannot be enforced.

In this instance, no convincing argument was advanced to the effect that the guarantee was invalid just because the underlying transaction was fundamentally different from that assumed by the forfaiters. There was no dispute as to the form of or signature to the aval. It seems likely, therefore, that the whole cost of settlement of the defaulted payments should have been borne by the guarantor, who, indeed, had no grounds not to pay *ab initio*. That the primary forfaiter agreed to share the cost is perhaps a consequence of a desire to avoid lengthy legal discussions as to the meaning and validity of an aval under the laws in the particular Middle-Eastern nation in which the guarantor was situated. This again emphasises the practical importance of establishing the jurisdiction and proper law governing an à forfait transaction at the outset and, if possible, of utilising a jurisdiction and the proper law of a nation well versed in such transactions.

APPENDIX I

Sample documentation

1. Offer or commitment letter

2. Promissory note

3. Bill of exchange

4. Aval on a bill of exchange
    Aval on a promissory note

5. Letter of guarantee

1.   Offer or commitment letter

London EC4
30 January 1985

Dear Sirs,

Re: À Forfait Finance – Ruritania

Thank you for your letter of 25 January 1985 in which you outlined a trade-backed transaction for which you seek quotations for à forfait finance.

In response, we make the following offer for the purchase, without recourse, of the related promissory notes.

Buyer:	Ruritania Engineering
Goods:	Lathes
Total sum to be financed:	DM2,068,000 by a series of six promissory notes maturing semi-annually
Period:	Last maturity not later than 30 April 1988
Delivery:	Goods – April 1985
	Documents – by 25 April 1985
Security:	Aval of Development Bank of Ruritania
Domicile of payment:	Ruritania
Interest:	9% per annum, compounded semi-annually, calculated on 365/360 basis and allowing five days of grace
Expiry of offer:	1 February 1985
Option period:	30 days from your acceptance of this offer
Option fee:	0.125% flat, payable immediately
Commitment fee:	Payable only if you are successful in obtaining the contract. 0.1% per month, payable monthly in advance from expiry of the option period until delivery of documents

Special require-ments:	Evidence of approval of foreign currency transfer by the State Bank of Ruritania and completion of promissory notes in accordance with the requirements of the Foreign Trade Documents Regulations 1981 issued by the Ruritanian Ministry of Foreign Trade

We hope that these terms meet with your approval.

Please signify your acceptance of these terms by signing and returning to us the copy of this letter attached.

Yours faithfully,

MIDLAND BANK AVAL LIMITED

2. Promissory note

· PROMISSORY NOTE ·

For eff.

Amount in figures

Place and Date of issue

On .... Name of month in letters .... 19 ....

against this promissory note I (We) promise to pay

To .... or Order

the sum of:

Amount in words

effective payment to be made in ....

FOR VALUE RECEIVED

payable at:

Signature of maker

Stamps on the reverse side

3. Bill of exchange

For eff. ....

At/On .... for value received, pay against this bill of exchange to

the order of .... the sum of

....

effective payment to be made in ....

This bill of exchange is payable at ....

Drawn on :

....
....

For Acceptance:

Per **Aval** for account of the drawee:

For........................... (drawer)

(Signature)

◁ **Back**

4.   Aval on a bill of exchange
     Aval on a promissory note

Aval on a bill of exchange

> PER AVAL for (name of drawee)
> (name and signature of guarantor)

Aval on a promissory note

> PER AVAL for (name of issuer)
> (name and signature of guarantor)

In both cases, the wording is written on the document itself.

5. Letter of guarantee

For value received (or for consideration received), we hereby irrevocably and unconditionally guarantee payment on behalf of

.... for the amount of ....

(name of obligor(s))   (amount in words)

for which the following.................... promissory notes/ bills of exchange have been issued

                  (number)

Amounts   Maturities

....

to the order of .... issued by ....

drawn by .... (name of beneficiary)

accepted by .... (name of obligor)

If .... (name of obligor)
does not pay, for any reason, we will pay at first demand even without

the note(s)/bill(s) having been protested, at the office of ....

                                      (domicile)

This guarantee is transferable and divisible and is subject to the Laws of ....
Claims under this letter of guarantee may be presented to us until one month after final maturity. When expired this letter of guarantee shall be considered as ineffective and shall be returned to us.

.... (name of guarantor)

.... (signature of guarantor)

Forfaiting rate indication sheet

 MIDLAND BANK AVAL   JANUARY 1985   Number 38

FORFAITING RATE INDICATIONS on basis of straight discount assuming six monthly repayments. 3-year transactions average life 1¾ years. 5-year transactions average life 2¾ years.

The indications below are for immediately available business; rates will be slightly increased for commitments of up to six months.

L.I.B.O.R. on 22.1.1985

periods	$	DM
6 months	8 13/16	5 15/16
1 year	9 5/8	6 1/16
2 years	10 7/8	6 1/2
3 years	11 1/4	6 7/8
4 years	11 1/2	7 1/8
5 years	11 7/8	7 5/16

EUROPE	period years	DM %	US$ %
Austria	5	6 1/2	9 1/2
Belgium	5	6 5/8	9 3/4
Denmark	5	6 5/8	9 3/4
Finland	5	6 1/2	9 1/2
France	5	6 5/8	9 3/4
Greece	5	7 1/8	10
Iceland	5	6 5/8	9 5/8
Ireland	5	7	9 7/8
Italy	5	6 3/4	9 3/4
Luxembourg	5	7	9 7/8
Netherlands	5	6 1/2	9 1/2
Norway	5	6 1/2	9 1/2
Portugal	5	7 1/2	10 3/8
Spain	5	6 3/4	9 3/4
Sweden	5	6 1/2	9 1/2

	period years	DM %	US$ %
Switzerland	5	6 1/2	9 1/2
UK	5	6 1/2	9 1/2
Turkey	3	8 7/8	11 7/8

ASIA AND AUSTRALASIA	period years	DM %	US$ %
Australia	5	6 1/2	9 1/2
China	5	6 1/2	9 1/2
Hong Kong	5	6 3/4	9 3/4
India	5	7	9 7/8
Indonesia	5	7 1/8	10
Japan	5	6 1/2	9 1/2
Malaysia	5	6 3/4	9 3/4
New Zealand	5	6 1/2	9 1/2
Papua New Guinea	5	7	9 7/8
Pakistan	3	9 1/8	12 3/8
Philippines	1	*	*
Singapore	5	6 1/2	9 1/2
South Korea	5	7	9 7/8
Sri Lanka	—	—	—
Taiwan	5	6 3/4	9 3/4
Thailand	5	6 7/8	9 7/8

AMERICAS	period years	DM %	US$ %
Brazil	—	—	—
Canada	5	6 1/2	9 1/2
Colombia	1	*	*
Cuba	1	*	*
Mexico	1	*	*

	period years	DM %	US$ %
USA	5	6 1/2	9 1/2
Venezuela	—	—	—

AFRICA	period years	DM %	US$ %
Angola	—	—	—
Cameroon	3	8 1/2	11 3/8
Gabon	3	8 1/2	11 3/8
South Africa	5	6 7/8	9 7/8
Tunisia	5	7 1/8	10

EASTERN BLOC	period years	DM %	US$ %
Bulgaria	5	7 1/8	10
CSSR	5	7	9 7/8
East Germany	5	7	9 7/8
Hungary	5	6 3/4	9 3/4
USSR	5	6 1/2	9 5/8

MIDDLE EAST	period years	DM %	US$ %
Abu Dhabi	5	7 1/8	10
Bahrain	5	7 1/8	10
Dubai	5	7 1/8	10
Egypt	3	11 3/8	14 3/8
Jordan	5	7 1/4	10 1/4
Kuwait	5	7 1/8	10
Saudi Arabia	5	7	9 7/8
Syria	1	*	*

* Subject to negotiation

Our indications are correct at the time of going to press inasmuch as they relate to the L.I.B.O.R. shown. During any particularly volatile period you are advised to relate our indications to L.I.B.O.R. on a given day. Our staff are always available to up-date indications, or give indications on countries not listed, in response to telephone or telex enquiries.

MIDLAND BANK AVAL LIMITED
135-141 Cannon Street London EC4N 5AY   01-623 8866   Telex 885501

APPENDIX III

Conversion of straight discount to semi-annual yield

Yield (per cent per annum) compounded semi-annually

Series*	1x6	2x6	3x6	4x6	5x6	6x6	7x6	8x6	9x6	10x6	11x6	12x6	13x6	14x6	15x6	16x6
Avge life (Yrs)	.50	.75	.99	1.23	1.47	1.70	1.93	2.17	2.39	2.62	2.85	3.07	3.29	3.51	3.73	3.95
5	5.1/8	5.3/16	5.3/16	5.1/4	5.5/16	5.3/8	5.3/8	5.7/16	5.1/2	5.9/16	5.5/8	5.5/8	5.11/16	5.3/4	5.13/16	5.7/8
5.1/8	5.1/4	5.5/16	5.3/8	5.3/8	5.7/16	5.1/2	5.9/16	5.5/8	5.5/8	5.11/16	5.3/4	5.13/16	5.7/8	5.15/16	6	6.1/16
5.1/4	5.3/8	5.7/16	5.1/2	5.9/16	5.9/16	5.5/8	5.11/16	5.3/4	5.13/16	5.7/8	5.15/16	6	6.1/16	6.1/8	6.3/16	6.1/4
5.3/8	5.1/2	5.9/16	5.5/8	5.11/16	5.3/4	5.13/16	5.7/8	5.7/8	5.15/16	6	6.1/16	6.1/8	6.3/16	6.1/4	6.5/16	6.3/8
5.1/2	5.5/8	5.11/16	5.3/4	5.13/16	5.7/8	5.15/16	6	6.1/16	6.1/8	6.3/16	6.1/4	6.5/16	6.3/8	6.7/16	6.1/2	6.9/16
5.5/8	5.13/16	5.13/16	5.7/8	5.15/16	6	6.1/16	6.1/8	6.3/16	6.1/4	6.5/16	6.3/8	6.1/2	6.9/16	6.5/8	6.11/16	6.3/4
5.3/4	5.15/16	5.15/16	6	6.1/8	6.3/16	6.1/4	6.5/16	6.3/8	6.7/16	6.1/2	6.9/16	6.5/8	6.11/16	6.13/16	6.7/8	6.15/16
5.7/8	6.1/16	6.1/8	6.1/16	6.1/4	6.5/16	6.3/8	6.7/16	6.1/2	6.9/16	6.5/8	6.3/4	6.13/16	6.7/8	6.15/16	7.1/16	7.1/8
6	6.3/16	6.1/4	6.3/16	6.3/8	6.1/2	6.1/2	6.9/16	6.11/16	6.3/4	6.13/16	6.7/8	7	7.1/16	7.1/8	7.1/4	7.5/16
6.1/8	6.5/16	6.3/8	6.5/16	6.1/2	6.5/8	6.11/16	6.3/4	6.13/16	6.7/8	7	7.1/16	7.1/8	7.1/4	7.5/16	7.7/16	7.1/2
6.1/4	6.7/16	6.1/2	6.1/2	6.11/16	6.3/4	6.13/16	6.7/8	7	7.1/16	7.1/8	7.1/4	7.5/16	7.7/16	7.1/2	7.5/8	7.11/16
6.3/8	6.9/16	6.5/8	6.5/8	6.13/16	6.7/8	6.15/16	7	7.1/8	7.3/16	7.5/16	7.3/8	7.1/2	7.9/16	7.11/16	7.13/16	7.7/8
6.1/2	6.11/16	6.3/4	6.3/4	6.15/16	7.1/8	7.1/8	7.1/8	7.5/16	7.3/8	7.1/2	7.9/16	7.11/16	7.3/4	7.7/8	8	8.1/16
6.5/8	6.13/16	6.7/8	6.7/8	7.1/8	7.1/4	7.1/4	7.3/16	7.1/2	7.1/2	7.5/8	7.3/4	7.13/16	7.15/16	8.1/16	8.3/16	8.1/4
6.3/4	6.15/16	7.1/16	7	7.1/4	7.3/8	7.7/16	7.3/8	7.5/8	7.11/16	7.13/16	7.15/16	8	8.1/8	8.1/4	8.3/8	8.1/2
6.7/8	7.1/8	7.3/16	7.1/8	7.3/8	7.1/2	7.9/16	7.1/2	7.13/16	7.7/8	8	8.1/16	8.3/16	8.5/16	8.7/16	8.9/16	8.11/16
7	7.1/4	7.5/16	7.5/16	7.1/2	7.5/8	7.3/4	7.11/16	7.15/16	8	8.1/8	8.1/4	8.3/8	8.1/2	8.5/8	8.3/4	8.7/8
7.1/8	7.3/8	7.1/2	7.7/16	7.11/16	7.3/4	7.7/8	7.13/16	8.1/8	8.3/16	8.5/16	8.7/16	8.9/16	8.11/16	8.13/16	8.15/16	9.1/16
7.1/4	7.1/2	7.5/8	7.9/16	7.13/16	7.15/16	8	8	8.5/16	8.3/8	8.1/2	8.5/8	8.3/4	8.7/8	9	9.1/8	9.5/16
7.3/8	7.5/8	7.3/4	7.11/16	7.15/16	8.1/16	8.3/16	8.1/8	8.1/2	8.9/16	8.11/16	8.13/16	8.15/16	9	9.3/16	9.5/16	9.1/2
7.1/2	7.11/16	7.7/8	7.7/8	8.1/8	8.1/4	8.5/16	8.5/16	8.5/8	8.3/4	8.13/16	9	9.1/8	9.1/4	9.3/8	9.1/2	9.11/16
7.5/8	7.13/16	8	8	8.1/4	8.3/8	8.1/2	8.7/16	8.13/16	8.7/8	9	9.1/8	9.5/16	9.7/16	9.9/16	9.3/4	9.15/16
7.3/4	7.15/16	8.1/8	8.1/8	8.3/8	8.1/2	8.5/8	8.5/8	9	9.1/16	9.3/16	9.5/16	9.1/2	9.5/8	9.13/16	9.15/16	10.1/8
7.7/8	8.1/16	8.3/16	8.5/16	8.9/16	8.11/16	8.13/16	8.3/4	9.1/8	9.1/4	9.3/8	9.1/2	9.11/16	9.13/16	10	10.1/8	10.3/8
8	8.3/16	8.5/16	8.7/16	8.11/16	8.13/16	8.15/16	8.15/16	9.5/16	9.3/8	9.9/16	9.11/16	9.7/8	10	10.3/16	10.3/8	10.9/16
8.1/8	8.5/16	8.7/16	8.9/16	8.13/16	9	9.1/8	9.1/8	9.3/8	9.9/16	9.11/16	9.7/8	10.1/16	10.1/4	10.3/8	10.5/8	10.13/16
8.1/4	8.7/16	8.5/8	8.11/16	8.7/8	9.1/8	9.1/4	9.1/4	9.9/16	9.3/4	9.7/8	10.1/16	10.1/4	10.7/16	10.9/16	10.13/16	11
8.3/8	8.5/8	8.3/4	8.7/8	9	9.5/16	9.7/16	9.7/16	9.3/4	9.15/16	10.1/16	10.1/4	10.7/16	10.5/8	10.13/16	11	11.1/4
8.1/2	8.3/4	8.7/8	9	9.1/8	9.7/16	9.9/16	9.9/16	9.15/16	10.1/16	10.1/4	10.7/16	10.5/8	10.13/16	11	11.1/4	11.1/2
8.5/8	8.7/8	9	9.1/8	9.5/16	9.9/16	9.3/4	9.3/4	10.1/16	10.1/4	10.7/16	10.5/8	10.13/16	11.1/16	11.1/4	11.1/2	11.11/16
8.3/4	9	9.5/16	9.5/16	9.7/16	9.3/4	9.15/16	10.1/16	10.1/4	10.7/16	10.5/8	10.13/16	11	11.1/4	11.1/2	11.11/16	11.15/16
8.7/8	9.1/8	9.7/16	9.7/16	9.3/4	9.7/8	10.1/16	10.1/4	10.7/16	10.5/8	10.13/16	11	11.1/4	11.7/16	11.11/16	11.15/16	12.3/16

Discount (per cent per annum)

* i.e. 1 note maturing in 6 months' time; 2 notes maturing in 6 months' time, etc.

Note : All conversions are rounded to the nearest 1/16 per cent.

Yield (per cent per annum) compounded semi-annually

Series*	1x6	2x6	3x6	4x6	5x6	6x6	7x6	8x6	9x6	10x6	11x6	12x6	13x6	14x6	15x6	16x6
Avge life (Yrs)	.50	.75	.99	1.23	1.47	1.70	1.93	2.17	2.39	2.62	2.85	3.07	3.29	3.51	3.73	3.95
9	9.7/16	9.9/16	9.3/4	9.7/8	10.1/16	10.1/4	10.7/16	10.5/8	10.13/16	11	11.3/16	11.7/16	11.11/16	11.15/16	12.3/16	12.7/16
9.1/8	9.9/16	9.11/16	9.7/8	10.1/16	10.3/16	10.3/8	10.9/16	10.3/4	11	11.3/16	11.7/16	11.5/8	11.7/8	12.1/8	12.3/8	12.11/16
9.1/4	9.11/16	9.7/8	10	10.3/16	10.3/8	10.9/16	10.3/4	10.15/16	11.3/16	11.3/8	11.5/8	11.7/8	12.1/8	12.3/8	12.5/8	12.15/16
9.3/8	9.13/16	10	10.3/16	10.3/8	10.9/16	10.3/4	10.15/16	11.1/8	11.3/8	11.9/16	11.13/16	12.1/16	12.5/16	12.9/16	12.7/8	13.3/16
9.1/2	10	10.1/8	10.5/16	10.1/2	10.3/4	10.7/8	11.1/16	11.5/16	11.1/2	11.3/4	12	12.1/4	12.9/16	12.13/16	13.1/8	13.7/16
9.5/8	10.1/8	10.5/16	10.7/16	10.5/8	10.7/8	11.1/16	11.1/4	11.1/2	11.11/16	11.15/16	12.3/16	12.7/16	12.3/4	13.1/16	13.3/8	13.11/16
9.3/4	10.1/4	10.7/16	10.5/8	10.13/16	11	11.3/16	11.7/16	11.11/16	11.7/8	12.1/8	12.7/16	12.11/16	13	13.5/16	13.5/8	13.15/16
9.7/8	10.3/8	10.9/16	10.3/4	10.15/16	11.3/16	11.3/8	11.5/8	11.7/8	12.1/16	12.3/8	12.5/8	12.7/8	13.3/16	13.1/2	13.7/8	14.3/16
10	10.1/2	10.3/4	10.15/16	11.1/8	11.3/8	11.9/16	11.13/16	12	12.1/4	12.9/16	12.13/16	13.1/8	13.7/16	13.3/4	14.1/8	14.1/2
10.1/8	10.11/16	10.15/16	11.1/16	11.1/4	11.1/2	11.3/4	12	12.3/16	12.1/2	12.3/4	13.1/16	13.5/16	13.11/16	14	14.3/8	14.3/4
10.1/4	10.13/16	11.1/8	11.3/16	11.7/16	11.5/8	11.15/16	12.1/8	12.3/8	12.11/16	12.15/16	13.1/4	13.9/16	13.7/8	14.1/4	14.5/8	15
10.3/8	10.15/16	11.1/4	11.3/8	11.9/16	11.13/16	12.1/8	12.5/16	12.9/16	12.7/8	13.1/8	13.7/16	13.13/16	14.1/8	14.1/2	14.7/8	15.5/16
10.1/2	11.1/16	11.3/8	11.1/2	11.3/4	12	12.3/8	12.1/2	12.3/4	13.1/16	13.3/8	13.11/16	14	14.3/8	14.3/4	15.1/8	15.9/16
10.5/8	11.1/4	11.9/16	11.11/16	11.7/8	12.1/8	12.9/16	12.11/16	12.15/16	13.1/4	13.9/16	13.7/8	14.1/4	14.5/8	15	15.7/16	15.7/8
10.3/4	11.3/8	11.3/4	11.13/16	12.1/16	12.5/16	12.3/4	12.7/8	13.1/8	13.7/16	13.3/4	14.1/8	14.7/16	14.7/8	15.1/4	15.11/16	16.3/16
10.7/8	11.1/2	11.7/8	11.15/16	12.1/4	12.1/2	12.15/16	13	13.5/16	13.5/8	14	14.5/16	14.11/16	15.1/8	15.1/2	16	16.7/16
11	11.3/4	12	12.1/8	12.3/8	12.5/8	13.1/8	13.3/16	13.1/2	13.13/16	14.3/16	14.9/16	14.15/16	15.5/16	15.3/4	16.1/4	16.3/4
11.1/8	11.15/16	12.3/16	12.1/4	12.1/2	12.13/16	13.1/4	13.3/8	13.11/16	14.1/16	14.3/8	14.3/4	15.3/16	15.9/16	16.1/16	16.1/2	17.1/16
11.1/4	12	12.5/16	12.7/16	12.3/4	13	13.7/16	13.9/16	13.7/8	14.1/4	14.5/8	15	15.3/8	15.7/8	16.5/16	16.13/16	17.3/8
11.3/8	12.1/8	12.7/16	12.9/16	12.7/8	13.3/16	13.5/8	13.3/4	14.1/16	14.7/16	14.13/16	15.1/4	15.5/8	16.1/8	16.9/16	17.1/8	17.11/16
11.1/2	12.1/4	12.5/8	12.3/4	13	13.3/8	13.13/16	13.15/16	14.1/4	14.5/8	15	15.1/2	15.7/8	16.3/8	16.7/8	17.3/8	18
11.5/8	12.3/8	12.3/4	12.7/8	13.3/16	13.1/2	14	14.1/8	14.7/16	14.7/8	15.1/4	15.11/16	16.1/8	16.5/8	17.1/8	17.11/16	18.5/16
11.3/4	12.1/2	12.15/16	13.1/16	13.1/2	13.11/16	14.1/8	14.5/16	14.5/8	15.1/16	15.1/2	15.15/16	16.3/8	16.7/8	17.7/16	18	18.5/8
11.7/8	12.5/8	13.1/16	13.3/16	13.5/8	13.7/8	14.5/16	14.1/2	14.13/16	15.1/4	15.11/16	16.1/8	16.5/8	17.1/8	17.11/16	18.5/16	18.15/16
12	12.3/4	13.3/16	13.3/8	13.13/16	14	14.1/2	14.11/16	15	15.7/16	15.15/16	16.3/8	16.7/8	17.7/16	18	18.5/8	19.5/16
12.1/8	12.15/16	13.3/16	13.1/2	13.15/16	14.3/16	14.11/16	14.7/8	15.3/16	15.5/8	16.1/8	16.5/8	17.1/8	17.11/16	18.5/16	18.15/16	19.5/8
12.1/4	13.1/16	13.5/16	13.5/8	14	14.3/8	14.3/4	15.1/16	15.7/16	15.7/8	16.3/8	16.7/8	17.3/8	17.15/16	18.9/16	19.1/4	20
12.3/8	13.3/16	13.1/2	13.13/16	14.1/8	14.1/2	14.7/8	15.1/4	15.5/8	16.1/8	16.9/16	17.1/8	17.5/8	18.1/4	18.7/8	19.9/16	20.5/16
12.1/2	13.5/16	13.5/8	13.15/16	14.5/16	14.11/16	15.1/16	15.7/16	15.11/16	16.5/16	16.13/16	17.3/8	17.15/16	18.1/2	19.3/16	19.7/8	20.11/16
12.5/8	13.1/2	13.3/4	14.1/8	14.7/16	14.13/16	15.1/4	15.5/8	15.7/8	16.9/16	17.1/16	17.9/16	18.3/16	18.13/16	19.1/2	20.1/4	21.1/16
12.3/4	13.5/8	13.13/16	14.1/4	14.5/8	15	15.3/8	15.13/16	16.1/16	16.3/4	17.5/16	17.13/16	18.7/16	19.1/16	19.13/16	20.9/16	21.7/16
12.7/8	13.3/4	13.15/16	14.7/16	14.13/16	15.3/16	15.9/16	16	16.1/2	17	17.1/2	18.1/16	18.11/16	19.3/8	20.1/8	20.15/16	21.13/16

Discount (per cent per annum)

* i.e. 1 note maturing in 6 months' time; 2 notes maturing in 6 months' time, etc.

Note : All conversions are rounded to the nearest 1/16 per cent.

Yield (per cent per annum) compounded semi-annually

Series*	1x6	2x6	3x6	4x6	5x6	6x6	7x6	8x6	9x6	10x6	11x6	12x6	13x6	14x6	15x6	16x6
Avge life (Yrs)	.50	.75	.99	1.23	1.47	1.70	1.93	2.17	2.39	2.62	2.85	3.07	3.29	3.51	3.73	3.95
Discount (per cent per annum)																
13	13.7/8	14.1/4	14.9/16	14.15/16	15.3/8	15.3/4	16.1/4	16.11/16	17.3/16	17.3/4	18.5/16	19	19.11/16	20.7/16	21.1/4	22.3/16
13.1/8	14.1/16	14.3/8	14.3/4	15.1/8	15.1/2	15.15/16	16.7/16	16.7/8	17.7/16	18	18.5/8	19.1/4	20	20.3/4	21.5/8	22.9/16
13.1/4	14.3/16	14.9/16	14.7/8	15.5/16	15.11/16	16.1/8	16.5/8	17.1/8	17.5/8	18.1/4	18.7/8	19.9/16	20.1/4	21.1/16	22	22.15/16
13.3/8	14.5/16	14.11/16	15.1/16	15.7/16	15.7/8	16.5/16	16.13/16	17.5/16	17.7/8	18.1/2	19.1/8	19.13/16	20.9/16	21.7/16	22.5/16	23.3/8
13.1/2	14.1/2	14.13/16	15.1/4	15.5/8	16.1/16	16.1/2	17	17.9/16	18.1/8	18.11/16	19.3/8	20.1/8	20.7/8	21.3/4	22.11/16	23.3/4
13.5/8	14.5/8	15	15.3/8	15.13/16	16.1/4	16.11/16	17.3/16	17.3/4	18.5/16	18.15/16	19.5/8	20.3/8	21.3/16	22.1/16	23.1/16	24.3/16
13.3/4	14.3/4	15.1/8	15.9/16	15.15/16	16.7/16	16.7/8	17.7/16	18	18.9/16	19.3/16	19.15/16	20.11/16	21.1/2	22.7/16	23.7/16	24.5/8
13.7/8	14.15/16	15.5/16	15.11/16	16.1/8	16.5/8	17.1/16	17.5/8	18.3/16	18.13/16	19.7/16	20.3/16	20.15/16	21.13/16	22.13/16	23.7/8	25
14	15.1/16	15.7/16	15.7/8	16.5/16	16.3/4	17.1/4	17.13/16	18.3/8	19	19.11/16	20.7/16	21.1/4	22.1/8	23.1/8	24.1/4	25.7/16
14.1/8	15.3/16	15.5/8	16	16.1/2	16.15/16	17.7/16	18	18.9/16	19.1/4	19.15/16	20.3/4	21.9/16	22.1/2	23.1/2	24.5/8	25.15/16
14.1/4	15.5/16	15.3/4	16.3/16	16.11/16	17.1/8	17.5/8	18.1/4	18.13/16	19.1/2	20.1/4	21	21.7/8	22.13/16	23.7/8	25.1/16	26.3/8
14.3/8	15.1/2	15.7/8	16.3/8	16.7/8	17.5/16	17.13/16	18.7/16	19.1/16	19.3/4	20.1/2	21.5/16	22.3/16	23.1/8	24.1/4	25.7/16	26.13/16
14.1/2	15.5/8	16.1/16	16.1/2	17	17.1/2	18.1/16	18.11/16	19.5/16	20.1/16	20.13/16	21.9/16	22.1/2	23.1/2	24.5/8	25.7/8	27.5/16
14.5/8	15.3/4	16.3/16	16.11/16	17.3/16	17.11/16	18.1/4	18.7/8	19.1/2	20.5/16	21.1/16	21.7/8	22.13/16	23.13/16	25	26.5/16	27.13/16
14.3/4	15.15/16	16.3/8	16.7/8	17.3/8	17.7/8	18.7/16	19.1/8	19.3/4	20.9/16	21.3/8	22.1/8	23.1/8	24.3/16	25.3/8	26.3/4	28.5/16
14.7/8	16.1/16	16.1/2	17	17.9/16	18.1/16	18.5/8	19.5/16	20	20.13/16	21.5/8	22.7/16	23.7/16	24.9/16	25.3/4	27.3/16	28.13/16
15	16.3/16	16.11/16	17.3/16	17.3/4	18.1/4	18.7/8	19.9/16	20.1/4	21.1/8	21.15/16	22.3/4	23.3/4	24.15/16	26.3/16	27.5/8	29.5/16
15.1/8	16.5/16	16.13/16	17.3/8	17.15/16	18.7/16	19.1/16	19.3/4	20.7/16	21.3/8	22.3/16	23	24.1/16	25.1/4	26.9/16	28.1/16	29.13/16
15.1/4	16.1/2	17	17.1/2	18.1/8	18.5/8	19.1/4	20	20.11/16	21.5/8	22.1/2	23.5/16	24.3/8	25.5/8	27	28.9/16	30.3/8
15.3/8	16.5/8	17.1/8	17.11/16	18.5/16	18.13/16	19.7/16	20.3/16	20.15/16	21.7/8	22.3/4	23.5/8	24.3/4	26	27.7/16	29.1/16	30.7/8
15.1/2	16.13/16	17.5/16	17.7/8	18.1/2	19	19.11/16	20.7/16	21.3/16	22.3/16	23.1/16	23.15/16	25.1/16	26.3/8	27.7/8	29.1/2	31.7/16
15.5/8	16.15/16	17.7/16	18	18.11/16	19.3/16	19.7/8	20.5/8	21.3/8	22.7/16	23.5/16	24.1/4	25.7/16	26.3/4	28.1/4	30	32
15.3/4	17.1/8	17.5/8	18.3/16	18.7/8	19.3/8	20.1/16	20.7/8	21.5/8	22.11/16	23.5/8	24.9/16	25.3/4	27.3/16	28.3/4	30.1/2	32.5/8
15.7/8	17.1/4	17.3/4	18.5/16	19.1/16	19.9/16	20.1/4	21.1/16	21.7/8	22.15/16	23.7/8	24.7/8	26.1/8	27.9/16	29.3/16	31.1/8	33.3/16
16	17.3/8	17.15/16	18.1/2	19.1/4	19.3/4	20.1/2	21.5/16	22.1/8	23.3/16	24.3/16	25.3/16	26.1/2	27.15/16	29.5/8	31.9/16	33.13/16
16.1/8	17.9/16	18.1/16	18.11/16	19.3/8	19.15/16	20.11/16	21.1/2	22.5/16	23.7/16	24.7/16	25.1/2	26.7/8	28.3/8	30.1/16	32.1/16	34.7/16
16.1/4	17.11/16	18.1/4	18.7/8	19.1/2	20.1/8	20.7/8	21.3/4	22.9/16	23.11/16	24.3/4	25.3/4	27.3/16	28.3/4	30.9/16	32.1/2	35.1/16
16.3/8	17.13/16	18.3/8	19	19.11/16	20.5/16	21.1/16	21.15/16	22.13/16	23.15/16	25	26.1/16	27.9/16	29.3/16	31.1/16	33.3/16	35.3/4
16.1/2	18	18.9/16	19.3/16	19.7/8	20.1/2	21.5/16	22.3/16	23.1/16	24.3/16	25.5/16	26.3/8	27.15/16	29.5/8	31.1/2	33.3/4	36.7/16
16.5/8	18.1/8	18.11/16	19.3/8	20.1/16	20.11/16	21.1/2	22.3/8	23.5/16	24.7/16	25.9/16	26.3/4	28.3/8	30.1/16	32	34.5/16	37.1/8
16.3/4	18.1/4	18.7/8	19.1/2	20.3/8	20.7/8	21.11/16	22.5/8	23.9/16	24.11/16	25.7/8	27.3/16	28.3/4	30.1/2	32.1/2	34.15/16	37.13/16
16.7/8	18.7/16	19	19.11/16	20.9/16	21.1/16	21.7/8	22.13/16	23.3/4	24.15/16	26.1/8	27.9/16	29.1/8	30.15/16	33.1/16	35.9/16	38.9/16
17	18.9/16	19.3/16	19.5/16	20.9/16	21.5/16	22.1/8	23.1/16	24.1/16	25.3/16	26.7/16	27.3/4	29.1/2	31.3/8	33.9/16	36.3/16	39.5/16

* i.e. 1 note maturing in 6 months' time; 2 notes maturing in 6 months' time, etc.

Note : All conversions are rounded to the nearest 1/16 per cent.

APPENDIX IV

Management reports

1. Interest-rate risk report for a forfaiter
2. Total currency position report for a forfaiter
3. Liquidity report for a forfaiter

1. Interest-rate risk report

CURRENCY:
DATE: 28 February 1985

Maturity	Assets maturing	Assets commencing*	Interest rates	Average earning rate	Liabilities maturing	Liabilities commencing*	Interest rates	Average borrowing rate
1–15 March 1985								
16–31 March 1985								
1–15 April 1985								
16–30 April 1985								
3 months								
4 months								
5 months								
6 months								
7 months–1 year								
1 year–2 years								
over 2 years								

*i.e. asset/liability expected to come on to the books – this will include options and commitments.

2. Total currency position report

DATE:

	Total £ equiv.	Sterling	DM £ = *	US$ £ = *	SFr £ = *	Yen Yen £ = *	Other £ = *
Net assets (liabilities)							
Options							
Commitments							
Swap purchases (swap sales)							
Net hedged position							
Forward currency purchases (forward currency sales)							
Net forward position							
Net total position							
Limit							
Excess							

* Sterling equivalent

3. Liquidity report

CURRENCY:

DATE: 28 February 1985

Maturity	Cash on hand	À forfait paper	À forfait commitments and options	Deposits	Loans	Interest commitments	Foreign currency contracts	Net position	Cumulative position
Demand Money									
1 – 15 March 1985									
16 – 31 March 1985									
1 – 15 April 1985									
16 – 30 April 1985									
May 1985									
June 1985									
July 1985									
August 1985									
September 1985									
October 1985									
November 1985									
*									
Undrawn credit facilities									

* Later maturities can be grouped in appropriate tranches

Index